8 Things No Kid Should Leave Home Without

by
Joe McGee

Harrison House
Tulsa, Oklahoma

14 13 12 11   10 9 8 7 6 5 4 3

8 Things No Kid Should Leave Home Without
ISBN 13: 978-1-57794-827-8
ISBN 10: 1-57794-827-0
Copyright © 2007 by Joe McGee
P.O. Box 691498
Tulsa, Oklahoma 74169-1498

Published by Harrison House, Inc.
P.O. Box 35035
Tulsa, Oklahoma 74153

Dedication

To Denise,

Sarah, Jessica, Corrie,

Tessa, Lauren, and John

for daily reminding me of what

truly is important in the journey of life.

A special thank you to my editor, Linda Schantz,

for her tenacity and her eye for detail.

Contents

Foreword

As a pastor, I have come to treasure the ministry of Joe McGee because of the impact he has on my families. His humorous manner and practical insight have helped countless families to make adjustments that have healed marriages, saved children, and strengthened local churches.

Take heed to *8 Things No Kid Should Leave Home Without*. This one is to be read and re-read as a manual for making disciples of those we must reach first—our own kids!

Pastor Willie George
Church On The Move
Tulsa, OK

Introduction

There's an old saying, "Marriage is forever; children are just passing through." Nothing could be more true. As parents, our job is to prepare our children to grow up and leave the nest.

Therefore shall a man leave his father and his mother, and shall cleave unto his wife: and they shall be one flesh.

Genesis 2:24 KJV

Our children are supposed to grow up and leave home in order to cleave to their mates.

Twenty years seems like a long time, but it's really not. Our time with our kids at home is so short, and we have so much to put into them before the time comes that they leave home to start their own families. We need to spend quality time loving them and teaching them, and we need to give them the things they need to be successful when they leave. When we look at our kids, we need to consciously remember that we're preparing them to leave.

I'll always be Dad to my kids, and we'll always have a relationship, but I'm preparing my son and my daughters for something beyond their time with me. As their Dad, the most important thing I need to do is to make sure my children are ready to go out into the world and do whatever God has called them to do.

I believe God has a plan for every person ever conceived. Whether we use them or not, He's placed gifts inside of every one of us, and He has an incredible plan to use each one of those gifts. When we fulfill the plans God has for us, we will be truly successful in life.

It takes some really special qualities to live out our full potential in life. However, I've noticed—and maybe you have too—that some people seem to be successful the moment they walk out the door. They seem to leave home with something so powerful inside them that they just can't be beaten down no matter what life throws at them.

All too often, though, most young people don't leave home with what they need to rise above life's challenges and to reach their full potential. They don't leave home with what it takes to make it in life.

Every time I've read a true success story I've noticed something: successful people have certain traits in common. Whether they've made their mark in athletics or politics, literature or science, the church or the corporate world, they all possess some of the same general characteristics. Some came from home with these things and others left with nothing, but they learned to develop these traits in adulthood. They got what they needed from the "school of hard knocks." Either way, all of them made an enormous impact on the world.

In this book I want to share with you the eight things that I believe consistently lead people to be successful in life. Ideally, parents will give these eight things to their children during their time at home. If every parent knew what to give their children so they could become the absolute best they could be, I believe most parents would do it. That's why I want to share these things with you.

Whether you're raising your own children or you want to achieve your full potential in your own life, this book is for you. If you're a parent, you can use this book as a resource as you raise your kids to achieve their God-given dreams. If you're someone who wants to reach your own potential and didn't come from home with some of these qualities, you can develop them in your own life and fulfill the plans God has for you.

I've had to wrestle with some issues in life because I didn't leave home with all of these things. Even if you didn't get everything you needed at home, I'm going to share some things you can do for yourself starting today. All you have to do is make a choice to change.

That's the great thing about God. His mercy is new every morning. Every day I get to start all over again! I don't care if I messed the day up so badly that I can't even believe it. I get to start all over again every morning.

God says, "Forget yesterday, Joe. We're going to erase it. You're going to repent over it and you get to start all over again today."

God is a redeemer and a restorer of the worst messes you've ever imagined. You might look at a mess you made and say, "There's no way this will ever turn out all right," but I've seen God do amazing things with situations that were hopeless. He says, "There's nothing I can't fix. There's nothing I can't redeem. Nothing."

In the chapters ahead, I'm going to cover eight things that enable young people to leave home with an advantage in life. No matter your vocation, location, ethnicity, religious background, or upbringing, these eight things will get you somewhere. They will also give you a better standard of living—a godly standard that will bring you His blessings. Each chapter will give you one key to living a better, more fulfilled life and how to give the same to each of your children. Here are the eight things no child should leave home without.

1

A Sense of Self-Worth

The first thing that no kid should leave home without is a sense of self-worth. Self-worth is something I've seen that gives young people a great advantage over others. Kids who have a tremendous sense of self-worth will go far in life.

The field of psychology has a lot of terms for this concept, including *self-esteem, emotional intelligence,* and *self-image.* All of these terms are used in reference to a person's sense of self-worth. They simply mean the way people feel about themselves. But a good sense of self-worth is based on more than just a feeling.

A low sense of self-worth can cause a lot of problems in life. As a parent, you are responsible to build your children's sense of self-worth and give them the confidence they need to succeed.

Success starts with a good sense of self-worth. Sometimes people associate their experiences or their possessions or their family tree with their worth. If they're proud of one of these things, they let it boost their confidence. But if they're ashamed of one of those things, they let it squash their sense of worth. People with a good sense of self-worth know they're valuable in spite of all these things. They base their value on something else.

An Example of Self-Worth

I've seen some extremely self-confident people come out of situations that would make others immensely depressed. For example, I remember a pastor I met who has a tremendous church that reaches thousands of people today. He was a big, burly guy and one day he told me, "Joe, I remember how I felt about myself when I was a kid. We lived in a shack, and when I say a shack I mean *a shack!* We had newspaper—not wallpaper—on the walls. We didn't even have electricity."

I was thinking, *Boy, that must've been rough!*

But he said, "You know, it never embarrassed me to invite buddies from my school to come home with me and spend the weekend. We'd go out fishing and hunting. We'd climb trees and swing from vines. I don't ever remember any boy not wanting to come back to my house. I had friends who loved it. I was never ashamed of where I was from. And since I wasn't ashamed, nobody else was either."

As a kid, this guy didn't have anything worth bragging about. His house was something most of us would be embarrassed to see. But self-confidence was something that was *in* him—not *around* him. And he's had that ever since. It was something his mom and dad put in him when he was a kid.

You Cannot Give What You Don't Possess

"'Love the Lord your God with all your heart and with all your soul and with all your mind.' This is the first and greatest commandment. And the second is like it: 'Love your neighbor as yourself.' All the Law and the Prophets hang on these two commandments."

Matthew 22:37-39

Jesus said the first commandment is to love God. The second is to love your neighbor as yourself. That's a commandment—not a suggestion. When we get to Heaven we'll all have to give an account for the way we lived our lives on this planet. God will ask us, "Did you spend your life loving your fellow man the way you loved yourself?"

Now the kicker to this thing is that each of us has to look in the mirror and ask, "Do I love me?" If I don't love myself, I can't love my neighbor. The second commandment, said in another way is, *"Love yourself—and love your neighbor just as much."* I can't love you any more than I love myself. A lot of people are trying really hard to love their neighbors without loving themselves. It doesn't work! If you can't love and accept who you are, then you can't love and accept anybody else.

> *...Husbands ought to love their wives as their own bodies. He who loves his wife loves himself.*
>
> Ephesians 5:28

A husband can't love his wife any more than he loves himself. *No one can give what they do not possess.* A husband who loves himself can love his wife because he has love to give. If you love yourself, you can love your neighbor. You have to have love on the inside of you to give it to someone else.

Your sense of worth has to focus on who you are on the inside. It has to come from the value that God saw in you when He sent Jesus to save you. Why did He do that? It wasn't because He thought you were perfect. It was because He loved you just the way you were.

None of us is perfect, but that doesn't change how valuable we are to God. Things on the outside change. Some days are great, and some days are not so great. Paul wrote about that.

> I know what it is to be in need, and I know what it is to have plenty. I have learned the secret of being content in any and every situation, whether well fed or hungry, whether living in plenty or in want.
>
> Philippians 4:12

In other words, "I know how to be full, and I know how to be half starved. I know my boat's sunk, but it doesn't matter what life throws my way. If I'm down, I'm going to float back up to the top tomorrow. This is temporary. Circumstances change. Who I am is not based on my circumstances. It's based on what God says about me."

Self-Worth Isn't Based on Appearances

A lot of people tie their sense of worth to their appearance, but it's important that we teach our kids that they're valuable for who they are on the inside. I had an experience one day that illustrated this point so clearly to me.

I was flying to St. Louis, and as I was getting ready for my flight, I saw that I would be sitting in seat 27A. *Twenty-seven A!* That was in the *very* back of the plane, in front of the bathroom, next to the window. Now, this was bad on many levels. First, I don't like a window seat because it boxes me in like a sardine. I like the aisle seat so I can stick my leg out and get a little room. Then, of course, back by the bathroom is *not* where you want to be on a long flight. (It smells back there!)

I was behind schedule because my first flight was late, so I ran to the plane. As I boarded, I saw that it was already packed with several large groups because it was Spring Break and kids were going home. When I reached row 27, I saw a rather large lady sitting in 27B. She wasn't an obese woman. She was just a very big woman—and I'm no little guy myself.

She had already pulled up the armrest between the seats to give herself a little more room, so by the time I got there she was sitting in her seat—and half of mine.

I stood there, looking at the remaining half of my seat by the window and feeling so bad for this lady. I thought, *Bless her heart,* and I said, "Ma'am, I'm sorry. I'm going to have to squeeze in there."

She smiled really big and got up, so I could scoot in. I got my seatbelt on quickly before she got in, and then she sat down again. Now, when I tell you we were sitting "cheek to cheek," I do not exaggerate a bit. We were *"cheek to cheek"!* But I learned a valuable lesson on this trip. This woman had something on the inside that I'd seen in other people before.

From the time I first saw her until the end of the flight, not one time did she apologize to me. She didn't say, "I'm sorry. I'm kind of taking up a lot of room." Not once did she feel the need to do that. She never stuttered or stammered. She just introduced herself, and we struck up a conversation. This woman was one of the most fun people I had sat by in an airplane in a long time. She was all excited about going home for Spring Break to see her family—including eight brothers and sisters.

By the time we got to St. Louis, we had a five-way conversation going on at the back of that plane. One of the flight attendants had even asked her for her name and address because she lived in St. Louis and wanted to get together with this woman over coffee.

Some people overcompensate when they feel bad about themselves, but that wasn't the case with this lady. She had us all feeling good on the back of that plane. Why? Because she felt good about herself inside. She liked herself. She was bold. She was confident. She didn't babble. She was a very intelligent woman.

When we were leaving the plane, people who didn't know her were hugging her neck because she made us all feel so good. When we got to the gate her family was there and they were jumping up and down like pogo sticks. (That was in the days when your family could meet you at the gate.)

When I saw them at that gate, I thought, *Wow! She's come from a family like that!* I learned something about parenting from them that day. You could tell that everybody in her family was loved. Nobody dwelled on anybody's faults or weaknesses or peculiarities. Everybody was accepted just as they were.

We can help our kids have a strong sense of self-worth by loving them unconditionally. That's how this gal had learned to love herself, and that love drew all of us in.

We all love to be around people who like themselves, and we don't like to be around people who don't like themselves. People who don't like themselves can make you feel really uncomfortable. It's like they have a hole in their soul. Since they don't like themselves they just assume others don't like them either. They will overcompensate for the lack of worth they feel for themselves by drawing constant attention and affirmation from those around them. It is as though they have to be continually propped up. They need to be the center of attention, tell the biggest story, talk the loudest, and do all the talking. They many times have a tendency to try to manipulate you and lie to you. They overcompensate because they don't feel good about themselves, and they project that onto other people.

Mark the perfect man, and behold the upright: for the end of that man is peace.

Psalm 37:37 KJV

People who know who they are in God's eyes are at peace with themselves. Instead of always walking into a room and *needing* a miracle, they walk into a room and *become* the miracle.

The people we like to be around are the people who love to be around people. They make us feel good. That's what the Body of Christ is supposed to be like. We're the salt, and we're the light. (Matt. 5:13.) We should love other people as we love ourselves. Some people leave home like that, but some of us need a little help with developing our self-worth.

What Poor Self-Worth Does

If you don't feel good about yourself, there are some negative things that will happen. There are consequences of low self-worth. I saw this in some of the kids in my school. They were intelligent. God had gifted them, but something stuck to their souls that made them feel bad about themselves. They thought the teachers or other people or circumstances were holding them down, but they weren't. *They* were holding themselves down by how they saw themselves. If you don't feel good about yourself, you'll never find the anchor to your own soul.

You can see it at your high school reunion. Some people you went to school with thirty years ago are still not comfortable with themselves. Some are still into self-abasement. They talk about what they can't do and how they're not good at it and how much stuff they've messed up. They're like the old woman who always wants to sit down and share about all her aches and pains. They're not asking for help. They just want to share the ugly.

You can only stand so much of that and then it's like a wet blanket. You walk away saying, "Dear Lord, I'm depressed."

But if you build your kids' self-worth, you can help them avoid these problems. Poor self-worth just naturally affects people.

1. Poor Self-Worth Creates Chameleons

Low self-worth will create chameleons—people who change color. If you don't feel good about you, then you don't know who you are. If you don't know who you are, then you'll change who you are to mimic whomever you're with so you will feel accepted. You adapt to wherever you are because you're a nobody. You don't have any backbone. I've watched good kids go bad because of this. Since they don't know who they are, they'll never stand up and oppose the crowd. They're very gullible, and they'll go wherever the crowd is going.

They don't know that God has a course just for them. They try to find their worth in everything around them. If everybody's excited, they'll get excited. If everybody's depressed, they'll get depressed. If everybody's mad, they'll be mad. That's what most vigilante groups are: a bunch of people who don't have a vision following somebody who does.

If you ask them, "What are you following for?" they'd have to say, "Because he got us all excited."

"Are you excited?"

"No, I'm not excited about anything, but he is. I'm just excited because he's excited."

Anybody who doesn't have convictions of his or her own will change like the wind. They're terrible friends to have. Don't be one!

Stand therefore, having your loins girt about with truth, and having on the breastplate of righteousness.

Ephesians 6:14 KJV

Therefore, brethren, stand fast, and hold the traditions which ye have been taught, whether by word, or our epistle.

2 Thessalonians 2:15 KJV

Submit yourselves therefore to God. Resist the devil, and he will flee from you.

James 4:7 KJV

Whom resist stedfast in the faith, knowing that the same afflictions are accomplished in your brethren that are in the world.

1 Peter 5:9 KJV

2. Low Self-Worth Makes You Wishy-Washy

Another consequence of having low self-worth is that it makes you wishy-washy. You can't make a decision. If you don't know who you are and you don't feel good about yourself, then you won't trust your own opinion. You'll always be asking yourself, "What if I make the wrong decision?" You'll always want to play it safe and never make a choice.

I've seen kids who don't know how to make decisions because they're always asking themselves, "What if make the wrong choice?" Well, you'll never know until you start. You've got to be willing to make a mistake.

In 1 Samuel 16:1, God told Samuel to go to the house of Jesse and anoint the next king. If Samuel had been scared of looking like a fool, he would never have found out who the king was supposed to be. God wouldn't tell him who it was. He would only tell him who it wasn't. Samuel had to go through seven embarrassments: "That's not the one...." Each time he passed one of Jesse's sons, he was committed. He was ready to anoint him, but God said, "Nope, not him." I wonder if Samuel was thinking, *Oh, that looked pretty dumb. I was just waving my hand.* But you know, Samuel would never have found out who it *was,* if he hadn't first found out who it *wasn't.*

If you're always worried about looking stupid, you'll never do anything. I've seen it happen to little kids, and I've seen it happen to adults. I don't care what age you are. Low self-worth will make you wishy-washy. If you're not confident in who you are, you're paralyzed and you won't make a decision.

This way of thinking starts early. Maybe somebody made fun of you when you were a kid. Maybe your daddy or your mama did. There could be a lot of reasons you feel this way.

Whatever happened to you in your life may not be your fault but now, as an adult, you're responsible to do something about it. Nobody else can. Nobody else can decide to develop your self-worth. You're responsible to lay those weights down and learn how to get rid of those things that somebody else tried to stick on you.

The wicked flee when no man pursueth: but the righteous are bold as a lion.

Proverbs 28:1 KJV

And now, Lord, behold their threatenings: and grant unto thy servants, that with all boldness they may speak thy word.

Acts 4:29 KJV

3. Low Self-Worth Invites Rejection

Low self-worth is almost like a magnet that draws rejection. When people are down on themselves, everybody else gets down on them too. It's like a self-fulfilling prophecy: "I don't feel good about me, and neither does anybody else."

I can still remember a kid in my school whose daddy wouldn't let him grow his hair out—and this was during the '60s! Everybody had long hair back then—except this kid. He had a burr. We'd say, "How come you don't let your hair grow out?" but his dad wouldn't let him.

That boy was always down on himself, and he attracted ridicule. If anybody was going to be made fun of that day, he was going to catch it. He could walk into a classroom and inspire ridicule. When you're thinking deep down inside, *I feel bad about me,* you pull other people into feeling bad about you too.

You can spot low self-worth because it starts in kids as bad thoughts about themselves. *I'm so dumb. I'm no good. I'm just not smart. I'm no good at English. I always make mistakes.* As parents we have to shut these thoughts down. There are people who don't even believe in the Bible who won't tolerate that.

> *...As he thinks in his heart, so is he.*
>
> Proverbs 23:7 NKJV

We can talk ourselves into anything if we say it long enough. That's a law of the kingdom of God.

I've seen people with the potential to be great athletes, musicians, or public speakers, but they say, "I can't do that. I'm not any good." And the people of God can be the most self-abasing bunch I've ever seen! God has called somebody to do something in the house of God, but they say, "No, I know I'm born again and filled with the Holy Spirit, but I can't...."

How are we going to take the world with that kind of thinking? Well, we're not, because the image of who we are in Christ isn't in our hearts yet. It has to come in degrees. It doesn't come in a flash. "For precept must be upon precept, precept upon precept; line upon line, line upon line; here a little, and there a little" (Isa. 28:10 KJV).

A good sense of self-worth has to be put in us from the outside. Everybody is born with the devil, the accuser of the brethren, telling us how stupid we are. We're told from the minute we're born what we can't do. "Don't do that." "Stop that." "Don't go there." "Don't eat that." We're told what we're not good at, what we've torn up, how we can't get it done, and why we're never right. No wonder we don't birth many world changers.

It's supposed to be different. When we were born, somebody was supposed to put the gospel in us. That's why the Bible says, "How can they believe unless they hear?" (Rom. 10:14). In other words, somebody has to put the Word in us from the outside. There's nothing in Joe McGee that was worth anything except what somebody put in me.

For our kids to be something, we have to put something in them. The words of Christ should dwell in them richly. (Col. 3:16 KJV.)

Without God there's nothing in you that's going to be any good. There's no self-confidence—nothing. The devil works on you the same way he works on everybody else to tell you how you're not going to amount to anything.

Until somebody can bash that lie with the truth from God's Word, the lie will win. You'll never attempt anything because you don't think you can. If you don't get around people that strike iron upon iron with you, who put good things in you and affirm you, you're never going to go anywhere in life. But as you see the value that God sees in you, you'll gain self-worth and stop listening to the devil's lies. And when you stop rejecting yourself, others will too.

...Let the weak say, I am strong.

Joel 3:10 KJV

I can do all things through Christ which strengtheneth me.

Philippians 4:13 KJV

4. Low Self-Worth Cripples Emotions

Low self-worth can cripple you emotionally. People with low self-worth are always thinking about themselves. I've seen this in intelligent people, people with degrees, people with high positions in ministry, and people in business. Everything is about them. They make terrible partners in marriage because they need continuous affirmation. They're like, "Give me, give me, give me."

I've seen this in marriage counseling. The husband says, "Well, I don't know if she likes me," and the wife says, "He asks me a million times, 'Do you like me?' and I'm thinking, *No, you drive me nuts!*"

"Am I okay? Please affirm me." People with a low sense of self-worth constantly want affirmation from everyone else, but they never give anything back.

Look not every man on his own things, but every man also on the things of others.

Philippians 2:4 KJV

You can size people up before you're married to see if they're like that. If you're a giver, don't hook up with somebody who's not a giver of time, praise, affirmation, money—everything. A person with low self-worth will drain a giver's well in a short amount of time.

For though by this time you ought to be teachers, you need someone to teach you again the first principles of the oracles of God; and you have come to need milk and not solid food.

Hebrews 5:12 NKJV

Milk is for babies. "Give me. Take care of me. Make me feel good" is the mindset of a baby. Low self-worth in Jesus Christ produces that.

People who come out of a home that produces self-worth in them will go out and change the world. They've found something that's eternal, and they're going to do something.

I always loved the story of Dr. Seuss going to twenty-seven different publishers trying to get a book published and their telling him he couldn't write books. He was driven. Finally a publisher said, "Yes, you can," and today over 200 million of his books have been printed. They're in more than fifteen languages.[1] If he'd been an emotional cripple, he would've said, "Oh, I'm sorry I took up your time," and settled for some menial job.

Robert Frost wrote poetry for many years before he became successful. Although he won four Pulitzer prizes and by the 1920s he was one of the most celebrated poets in America, he was thirty-nine years old when his first collection of poems was published.[2]

He knew who he was inside. It wasn't outside of him. For years there was nothing to encourage or affirm him from outside of himself. It was inside, and it drove him.

If you're ashamed of yourself, constantly needing affirmation from other people, the devil will keep you poor and ashamed because people can't carry you where God wants you to go.

5. Low Self-Worth Squanders Potential

When a person feels little about himself, he makes little choices about his life. He squanders his potential by setting little goals, settling for little jobs, and making friends with little people because he reasons, "I'm little, and this is all I deserve."

God doesn't want us to think that way. He has *big* plans for us. I believe that God loves a bold attitude—not arrogance, but boldness. David was a man after God's own heart (Acts 13:22), and David told Goliath, "I'm going to whip you." (See 1 Sam. 17:45-47.)

Saul told David, "You're not a man of war. You're a sheep-herder."

David answered, "Yeah, but I've got something in here that you don't know about. I don't need your armor or your encouragement. I'm about to whip the snot out of Goliath and take his head off."

David was confident because he'd found something to be confident in. He'd spent hours in fellowship with God out there with the sheep. He thought, *I don't need anybody's approval. I've got God's approval.*

I've seen kids come out of homes with natural self-confidence who achieved things that believers would never even attempt. So many Christians blame God when they don't reach their potential. They make excuses when they try something that fails, saying, "That must not have been God." How many believers have you heard say that?

Somebody asks, "I thought you said you were going to do this."

And they say, "Well, yeah, I was, but it just wasn't God."

That sure takes the pressure off! That's also a quick way to go from a winner to a wimp! There's no backbone in that. You have to know who you are and have some self-worth inside of you to reach your full potential.

For I know the thoughts that I think toward you, saith the LORD, thoughts of peace, and not of evil, to give you an expected end.

Jeremiah 29:11 KJV

Call unto me, and I will answer thee, and shew thee great and mighty things, which thou knowest not.

Jeremiah 33:3 KJV

6. Low Self-Worth Makes Moral Pushovers

If you don't have a backbone, you sure aren't going to have one when it comes to morality. When you don't feel good about yourself, you'll do some dumb, sinful stuff. I know because I've been there. You feel like a dog to begin with, and you're looking for someone or something to give you some worth. You'll look to the flesh to get it if you don't have it in the spirit.

The way to avoid being a moral pushover and all of the terrible consequences of sin that follow that is to start building up your self-worth. Every day we need to make a choice.

Awake to righteousness, and sin not; for some have not the knowledge of God....

1 Corinthians 15:34 KJV

Paul said, "I've got to die daily to the flesh" (1 Cor. 15:31). Every day we need to choose to seek God and get our daily manna. This day is supposed to be better than yesterday—not worse. We're supposed to keep moving forward, not falling down because we don't have any moral strength.

How To Build Self-Worth in Your Kids

The most important thing our kids need in order to have self-worth in life is a relationship with God Almighty. They get that by our telling them stories from the Bible.

God said, "I know that Abraham will teach his children, his children's children, and all those of his household. Therefore, I will bring these blessings on him." (See Gen. 18:19.) God blessed Abraham because He knew he'd pass two things on to his children: the blessing and the way he got it.

Abraham didn't start out with this great relationship with God. *His relationship with God started with the stories he had heard.* Abraham had heard about what God had done because Noah's descendants were still around when Abraham was born. They passed on the stories about the Flood and what happened when they landed. Abraham knew there was a God, he believed in God, but he didn't have a personal relationship with Him. He feared Him, but they didn't visit every day.

Then one day God showed up and had a conversation with him: "Abraham, we're going to have a relationship." The first thing God said Abraham had to do was take a trip. God said, "I want to take you to a land you've never been to." (See Gen. 12:1-3.) There wasn't a lot of sacrifice in that. All Abraham had to do was move. So he obeyed.

Then he started obeying God in other things, and all of a sudden God told him he was going to have a son. (Gen. 15:4.) He was thinking, *Well, I can't do that. That's not physically possible, because my wife is past child-bearing age.* But he decided to believe God anyway (v. 6.), and the next thing you know, he had a baby boy. Then God showed up and asked him to sacrifice that kid. (See Gen. 22.) Notice that every step required more faith, because a relationship with God builds over time. It takes time to get to know God, and the way you get to know Him is by reading and hearing the stories of the Bible.

For he established a testimony in Jacob, and appointed a law in Israel, which he commanded our fathers, that they should make them known to their children: That the generation to come might know them, even the children which should be born; who should arise and declare them to their children: That they might set their hope in God, and not forget the works of God, but keep his commandments: And might not be as their fathers, a stubborn and rebellious

*generation; a generation that set not their heart aright, and
whose spirit was not stedfast with God.*

Psalm 78:5-8 KJV

There are eleven different places in the Bible where
parents are commanded to tell their children the stories
of the Bible. That's how we start to build our children's
self-worth. These stories were left for our example, and
they fill us with hope. They tell us that God works with
sinners, weak people, people who mess up—even
people who mess up badly. God works with everybody,
redeems everybody, saves everybody, loves everybody,
gives to everybody, and forgives everybody. He's a
giving, loving God.

If I've got all these stories in me, I know that whatever
happens to me, I can get back up if I fall down and I can
keep moving because God is with me and He's for me.
The people who make it in life are the people who know
how to get back up when they get knocked down. That's
because they know who they are inside. If we've got a
relationship with God, and we know what He's done in
the past, like Abraham, we'll make it.

Relationships Take Time

When I started dating my wife, Denise, I was so nervous I was scared spitless. I thought, *I'm going to have to get some hair on my lip to ask this woman out.*

I remember the first time I called her on the telephone. I asked, "Is Denise there?"

Her mother answered the phone and said, "Yes, just a minute," and Denise came to the phone.

I said, "Is this Denise Campbell?"

She said, "Yes."

I said, "Denise, this is Joe McGee." I introduced myself, and we talked for a while. After that, we went out two or three times.

About a week later I called her, she answered the phone, and I said, "Denise?"

She said, "Yes."

And I said, "This is Joe." Then we dated a little while longer, and after about three months, I called her and she answered the phone and I said, "Hey, Denise."

"Yeah."

"It's me."

And after a while I could call and just say, "Hey."

And she just said, "Hey," because we knew each other.

You know, the longer you walk with God, the easier it is to talk with Him. There's no need for any formal introductions. You don't have to give your whole name, address, and serial number. You know each other. You know what each other thinks, likes, and doesn't like.

When we teach our children Bible stories, we're introducing them to their Father God. It's the first step toward building a personal relationship with Him, which is the only thing that will give them true and lasting self-worth. This takes time! As your kids grow you're helping them to get to know God and introducing them to their Lord and Savior Jesus Christ. When they know God through Jesus, they become firmly established in who they are and why they're on this planet. Then they'll set their hope in Him forever. (Ps. 78:7.)

A child with self-worth is a child full of hope. They know, "Even if I mess up, even if I flunk a grade, I still have hope. There's still a God in Heaven. He still loves me and has a plan for my life, and nothing's going to change that." Today is not the culmination of my life; it's just one day in the journey in my life. The sun will come up in the morning. If we have that truth in us, our self-worth will soar.

We Can Come Boldly to the Father

I remember my son John showing me a scar a few years ago.

I said, "Where'd you get that?"

He said, "Well, I was running through the woods and I tripped and fell over a big stump."

I said, "Wow, Son, that's a pretty ugly scar. Did your mom put some medicine on it?"

"No, I didn't tell Mom, because I didn't want her to tell you."

"Why didn't you want to tell me, Son?"

"I was afraid you'd get mad because I was chasing the chickens, and you told me not to do that."

John used to chase chickens like dogs chase cats. I don't know what it was. He just wanted to see if he could catch them. But the whole time he was recovering from that injury, he didn't tell anybody. He was trying to doctor himself for days, and now he had this ugly scar.

How do you think it made me feel as a father, that when my son hurt himself he felt like he couldn't run to me for help? It wasn't because he was afraid of me. He just knew I wasn't going to be pleased.

That was powerful, and it taught me something about our relationship with God. Sometimes we're afraid to go to Him because we've messed up, but He says we can run "boldly unto the throne of grace"—even when we've sinned like a dog (Heb. 4:16). You have to have some strong self-worth to run boldly to somebody when you've offended him in a big way.

God wants us to know that our worth is based on what He gave us through Jesus. We're worth a ton. That doesn't mean God won't confront us when we sin, but when we mess up He's an encourager. When David sinned with Bathsheba, God sent a prophet to him to confront him—not because God was mad at him, but to save him from his sin because God loved him.

The Bible says that if we don't discipline our children, we treat them as if they're illegitimate because we don't care what happens to them. (Heb. 12:8.) But if we love them we're going to confront them and teach them about God's forgiveness and His holiness.

If you'll read Bible stories to your kids and teach them how God loves them and values them, they'll know, "I'm worth a lot because God loves me. If I fall, I'll get back up and try again because He forgives me and He'll lead me so that I can succeed."

Affirmation Builds Self-Worth

As we build our kids' self-worth by teaching them Bible stories and leading them to a personal relationship with Jesus Christ, we also need to give them affirmation. Affirmation is showing our love and approval through our words. Words are powerful.

> Death and life are in the power of the tongue: and they that love it shall eat the fruit thereof.
>
> Proverbs 18:21 KJV

Romans 13:1-8 says that everyone in a position of authority—whether it is a parent, an employer, a military commander, or a government official—has two responsibilities. *First,* we are to confront and punish what is evil. And *second,* we are to praise that which is good.

Half of all the time authorities spend doing their jobs should be used for praising the good that's around them.

That's a spiritual law. It accelerates whatever is good. It's like pouring gasoline on a fire. Whatever is good is accelerated by words of praise.

Affirmation is vital. God affirmed Jesus before He faced the devil. He said, "This is My Son, and by the way, I'm really pleased with Him." (See Matt. 3:17 and 17:5.) God handed out affirmation to His Son, and He wants parents to affirm their kids too. Unfortunately, a lot of people didn't receive the affirmation they needed from their parents when they were young. I do believe that God will send people to affirm and encourage us, even though we may not have received it from our own parents. God is really big on encouragement. He'll send us affirmation because He knows we need it to build our self-worth.

Encourage Yourself

Another way to receive affirmation is to speak it over yourself. We can talk to ourselves, and we can choose to encourage ourselves or to be depressed. If you don't have anybody else to affirm you, then you have to affirm yourself. The Bible tells us, "David encouraged himself in the Lord" (1 Sam. 30:6). Tell your kids that. Tell them,

"You're just going to have to talk to yourself and say, 'Nobody else wants to talk nice about me, so I'll just talk nice about myself.'"

People aren't always going to be around to pat you on the back. You have to choose to keep your face buried in the mirror of God's Word, so you don't forget what manner of man you are. You're blessed. As your soul prospers, so your health and finances prosper. Everything is tied to how you think. So we have to watch how we think. We have to watch what we feed on, because what we feed on determines what we think.

Teach your kids that the best way to encourage yourself is to go to the Bible and start quoting it. Say, "I'm the redeemed of the Lord. I'm the apple of His eye. I'm the head and not the tail, above and not beneath." (See Ps. 107:2; Ps. 17:8; Deut. 28:13.) Just start saying what God says about you, and you'll speak life back into your own soul.

Many of us say, "I'm so ugly. I'm so dumb." We need to be saying, "God made me, so I've got to be good-looking." If other people say we're too short, too fat, too tall, too skinny—or whatever—they don't know what they're talking about. We can say, "God made me like this, so He must like me. I've got to be good-looking in God's eyes." God has six-winged angels that have eyeballs looking in every direction, and He thinks they're pretty. (Rev. 4:8.) He has to think I'm good-looking!

You have to say what the Word says about you, or you'll repeat the lies that the devil and other people say about you. And if you want people to say good things about you, sow some seed and say good things about somebody else. You'll reap "good measure, pressed down, and shaken together, and running over" (Luke 6:38).

Accept Your Kids the Way They Are

People whose parents accept them the way they are have a strong sense of self-worth. I don't mean that parents should accept their kids' sin, but they should still accept their kids and affirm them while correcting them when they do make mistakes.

For example, if a kid wrecks the car because he snuck out of the house and stole it, then the parents have a choice right there. The child should be punished because that's what happens when a kid sins, but *how* the parents issue that punishment is really critical. Dad and Mom can either discipline with love and accept the child or they can criticize the kid and call him stupid.

As parents, we have to remember that words stick. Punishment will pass; it's temporary. But words are forever. What we say brings life or death for a very long period of time. We can make that spiritual law work *for* us and not against us by making sure that we affirm our kids when we discipline them. We can speak life over them even when they are mixed up and messed up. Speaking words of life that are based on the Word of God will set their course for success because our kids will know that total victory is just one step away from failure.

No kid should leave home without a strong sense of self-worth. It will help to point them toward success in life. As a parent, you can build your kids' self-worth by telling them Bible stories that fill them with hope in God and by giving them sincere words of affirmation. When you do these two things, you'll give them an advantage in life and help them reach their God-given potential.

2

Vision

Besides having a good sense of self-worth, the people who have an advantage in life are people of vision. We know from the Bible that God is a God of vision. Isaiah 46:10 says that He knows and declares the end from the beginning, so He sees ahead and speaks what He wants to happen in the future.

Where there is no vision, the people perish.

Proverbs 29:18 KJV

Sometimes people can live without really living. It's like they're perishing even though all their vital organs are working. You have to know why you're here. There has to be a reason for your life. You can't just be another person, another number, taking up space. If that's all you think you are, you won't try anything and you'll have no hope.

You have to raise your kids to think, *I'm here for something really important. My name may not be in the encyclopedia, but God created me to do something great. Maybe it's not today, maybe it's not until the last day I take a breath, but eventually I'm going to make a mark here on this planet.*

Kids don't just automatically think this way about themselves. As a parent, you have to put that into them. And if *you* didn't get that as a kid, you have to put that in yourself too. How do you do that? You do it by looking at the right things.

> *While we look not at the things which are seen, but at the things which are not seen: for the things which are seen are temporal; but the things which are not seen are eternal.*
>
> 2 Corinthians 4:18 KJV

The goal is to stop focusing on what we can see and to focus instead on something we can't see—namely, God's plan for our lives. The devil wants us to look at what we can see in the natural. He wants to keep us locked into all our limitations, faults, and weaknesses.

But the way we stay locked into the unseen is to realize that the things that we can see are all temporary.

Everything changes. Maybe it goes from bad to worse, or maybe it goes from bad to better, but everything changes. When we're focusing on the things that are eternal, we can override what's happening in the natural with the vision God has given us for our lives.

Let me tell you what a vision is. A vision is something that's not seen yet. God says, "You're going to perish if you can't see what you don't see yet." A vision of God's purpose for your life will lead you all the way through life until you draw your last breath.

Vision Outlives Us

I am fascinated by the power of vision when I go to places like Disney World. I know people are really taking shots at Disney for this or that, but there isn't a thing at Disney World that God didn't give someone a gift to create. Do you think some human thought up all that stuff?

I heard a story about a reporter who managed to get in to do a last interview with Walt Disney just before he died. The reporter had been trying to get in for weeks, and the night before Disney died a nurse let him go up to Walt's room.

Disney was so weak that he couldn't sit up or talk in a normal voice, so he motioned to the reporter to lie down on the bed next to him so he could whisper in his ear. The reporter knew Walt was dying and Walt knew he was dying too.

The reporter wanted to ask some basic questions like, "Do you feel like you have fulfilled your life?" and "Do you think you helped people with your foundations?" But instead, Walt used the ceiling like a drawing board and talked for thirty minutes about his new park in Florida, Disney World. He explained what he was going to build, where everything was going to be, what it was going to do, and what it was going to look like.

See what happens when a man has a vision? Walt Disney is gone now, but his vision is still here.

How To Get a Vision

It is written, "No eye has seen, no ear has heard, no mind has conceived what God has prepared for those who love him"—but God has revealed it to us by his Spirit.

1 Corinthians 2:9

The only way to get a vision is to get it from God. He has planned great things for each of us, but we have to ask Him to reveal them to us. God says, "You do not have because you do not ask" (James 4:2). To get a vision, we have to ask for it. We have to say, "God, what do You have planned for me?"

Psalm 139:16 says that His plan for us was written in a book before we were ever born. God says His plans for you are great and mighty. He says He'll prosper you and give you a future and a hope, and not one that will harm you. He says if you would ask Him, He'll reveal His plans to you and to your children. (Jer. 33:3; Jer. 29:11; Deut. 29:29.) A vision is not just for you in your lifetime. It's to build something that lasts forever.

Have you ever had someone try to explain something to you and finally you saw it? Second Corinthians 4:4 says that Satan has blinded the minds of unbelievers. Jesus said, "In seeing, they don't see" (Matt. 13:13).

Jesus spoke in parables because His audience was spiritually blind. The people were looking, but they didn't see it. He said to His disciples, "Boys, did you understand what I taught today?"

They said, "Nope, we didn't see it."

He said, "Well, it's kind of like a farmer. You understand farming, don't you?"

"Yep."

He would always use something natural that they could see to explain something they couldn't see. Then He'd say, "Do you understand?"

And they'd say, "Oh, we see it now."

Jesus knew that if His disciples had a vision of the kingdom, it would keep them going the rest of their lives. Your kids are the same way. If you pray with them and ask God to show them the vision for their lives and drive out the devil with the truth of the Word, your kids will get the vision for their lives from God and run with it.

Vision Will Lead You

In the Old Testament Joseph had a vision that he was going to be famous. People were going to bow down to him. When he had this dream from God, he was the runt of the family, but he knew that one day he was going to become the top dog.

He had a vision, and it kept him going for twenty years. His brothers lied about him, hated him, despised him, and almost killed him. (Gen. 37.) Potiphar's wife lied about him, and he had to go to jail for it. (Gen. 39.) He helped Pharaoh's baker and butler while they were in prison with him, he begged them not to forget him when they got out, but he stayed in that jail for years for a crime he didn't commit. (Gen. 40.) Through all that, his vision took him onward and upward. He didn't sit in his jail cell feeling sorry for himself. The Bible says, "And the keeper of the prison committed to Joseph's hand all the prisoners that were in the prison; and whatsoever they did there, he was the doer of it" (Gen. 39:22 KJV).

It's as though Joseph was saying, "God gave me a vision, and I don't care what you do to me. I'm going where God said I'm going." He didn't throw a fit and curse his brothers. When Potiphar's wife accused him, he didn't yell, "That wicked woman lied about me!" The Bible has no record that he even opened his mouth. Why? Because God had given him a vision, and he knew nobody could stop him from fulfilling God's plan for his life.

That's what kept Paul going when his boat was sinking. God sent an angel to remind Paul, "The boat you're on is going down, but you won't die. I told you before, and I just want to remind you again. You won't die until you do everything I said you're going to do. You're going to preach to the Gentiles. You're going to preach in front of kings." (See Acts 27:23-25.)

Vision led Joseph, vision led Paul, and vision will lead you and your kids. Kids with a vision can take failure because they know they're not through until the vision is completed.

When this is your attitude, you don't get paralyzed with indecision and fear. You take life for all it's worth to pursue the vision. Every day you think, *I've got this vision, and I'm going to do something.*

A Vision Changes Everything

When Paul was on the road to Damascus he got knocked off his horse and a very interesting thing happened: his eyes were blinded. He had a vision, not with his natural eyes but with his spiritual eyes. He was blind, but he saw something nobody else saw and it changed his life. (See Acts 9:1-19.)

Even if you have no eyesight you can still see. Your spirit can see. That's why God said, "If you don't see spiritually, you're going to perish" (Prov. 29:18). The devil will throw natural things at you to try to shut you down, distract you, and make you give up. But if you can see with your spiritual eyes, you won't perish.

If you can't see it in your heart, you can't possess it. You can only have what you can see. So how do you see yourself five years from now? Do you see yourself stronger or weaker? Richer or poorer? Staying where you are or going somewhere? Has the devil put a vision in you that you're never going to change? If so, then stop and consider that you're looking at life with natural eyes instead of spiritual eyes. There's little in the natural to make you think things would change for the better. The devil is going to throw circumstances at you. He's going to buffet you with the tests and trials of life. Jesus said these would come to every one of us. (Luke 6:46.) If you don't have spiritual insight, your natural eyesight will depress you and you'll give up and pull back. God says, "I have no pleasure in those who pull back." (See Heb. 10:38.)

I'm where I am today because I saw myself here. I didn't see it in the natural, but I knew it was coming. God showed my wife and me back in 1975 that one day I was going to travel the country and teach families. I used to get F's in oral book reports. I stuttered and my tears ran like a faucet when I tried to speak in public. But if I had concentrated on the past, I wouldn't have gotten to where

I am today. If I had meditated on how I fought all the time in school or that I was afraid of flying in an airplane, I wouldn't be traveling or teaching anybody now.

When the vision for my ministry came from God, everything changed. In a night, in a moment, in a time of prayer, I got a vision of the future. I saw something that in the natural couldn't possibly be possible. It was too big. I thought, *That's crazy!* When I prayed it out that night I told Denise, "Isn't that the stupidest thing you've ever heard of in your life? That wasn't God. Forget that deal."

At first, my head picked up what my spirit saw and it shut it down. My mind said, "That's not going to happen." But it did because God immediately started working on me. The seed was out, and He began to water it and cultivate it, until one day it was planted deep into my heart. I could see it and I began to act upon it, until finally, I was living the vision.

God can do anything with us if we will just open our spiritual eyes, see what He sees, and do what He tells us to do. We're on a journey that just keeps getting better and better. We're going from faith to faith and from glory to glory.

But the path of the [uncompromisingly] just and righteous is like the light of dawn, that shines more and more (brighter and clearer) until [it reaches its full strength and glory in] the perfect day [to be prepared].

Proverbs 4:18 AMP

Jacob's Vision

In Genesis 30, we read about a man who understood vision. His name was Jacob. Jacob had a twin brother named Esau. Esau was the oldest, so he was supposed to get the inheritance, the double blessing, from their dad. The firstborn was supposed to get twice as much stuff. Then he was responsible, as the head of the family, for others in the family who had no stuff.

Esau didn't want the responsibility. He said, "I'll just take my own stuff. I don't want to be responsible for everybody else." Before they were born, God knew what they would do. He said, "Jacob I have loved, but Esau I have hated" (Rom. 9:13). He knew Esau placed no value on the birthright and the blessing of God, but Jacob did.

Jacob wanted that blessing. It wasn't just the stuff that he wanted. He wanted to be the head because he wanted to be responsible. The Bible says, "If anyone sets his heart on being an overseer, he desires a noble task" (1 Tim. 3:1). Why? That person is saying, "I want to be responsible, God. In the natural I know I can't meet these needs, but I know that if I'll be responsible, You'll flow through me to meet these needs." The one who says that has some self-esteem and some vision.

That's the position Jacob would take in his family. With his mama in on the deal, he snuck into his blind father's graces and got Isaac to give him the blessing. Jacob got it legally. Some people say that he stole it, but he didn't. He bought it for a bowl of soup.

Nevertheless, when he had gotten the birthright and the blessing, Jacob thought, *Esau's going to kill me!* So he ran off to his uncle Laban's place. While he was there, he saw one of Laban's daughters, Rachel, and fell madly in love with her.

Laban said, "You can have her if you work for me seven years."

You know the story. Jacob proceeded to work seven years for Rachel, and on the wedding night Laban sent her older sister Leah into Jacob's tent. Then he made Jacob work another seven years to get Rachel. After working for his uncle all those years and being tricked by him, Jacob realized that Laban had no vision for himself. He was just an old heathen, and the only vision he had was the one Jacob gave him, so Laban held onto Jacob for all he was worth. But then Jacob decided it was time to go home and take his chances with Esau.

After Rachel gave birth to Joseph, Jacob said to Laban, "Send me on my way so I can go back to my own homeland. Give me my wives and children, for whom I have served you, and I will be on my way. You know how much work I've done for you." But Laban said to him, "If I have found favor in your eyes, please stay. I have learned by divination that the Lord has blessed me because of you."

Genesis 30:25-27

Do you know where Laban saw himself five years in the future if this boy didn't stay? He saw himself broke. He had no vision of his own. He knew Jacob had a vision, and he wanted to keep him around.

Jacob wrestled for his vision. He wrestled with his brother for it. He wrestled with the angel all night for it. He wanted the blessing so badly that he said, "I'm not letting you go until you bless me. I want it, and I want it all" (Gen. 32:24-26).

God said, "Man, I like this guy," and He gave him a vision that would bring him and his descendents blessing forever. In order to fulfill that vision, though, Jacob had to get away from Laban. But every time he tried, Laban would say, "Don't leave. I'll be broke if you go."

Set Your Own Salary

In desperation, Laban said to Jacob,

"Name your wages, and I will pay them."

Genesis 30:28

Have you ever had anybody tell you, "Set your own salary"? That's basically what Laban said to Jacob: "We want to keep you here. Name your salary."

But Jacob said, "But God wants to *really* bless me. You want to bless me a little bit. Somebody else wants to bless me a bunch." We need to start thinking like that.

In Genesis 30:29-30, Jacob tells Laban:

"You know how I have worked for you and how your livestock has fared under my care. The little you had before I came has increased greatly, and the Lord has blessed you wherever I have been. But now, when may I do something for my own household?"

Does Jacob have some self-worth or what? Here's a kid who feels good about himself!

Can you imagine going to work and saying, "When I showed up here, you didn't have anything going on. But since I've been here, you are blessed." What kind of attitude is that for an employee? That's a good one (but you don't need to go say that if you like your job)!

"If I leave, you're going to be in trouble. Because I brought the blessing with me, and I'm taking it when I go." Now don't go tell your boss that! But that's basically what Jacob said: "Look, I've worked for you and I've blessed you, but now I need to get my own thing going."

Laban said, "What shall I give thee?" (Gen. 30:31 KJV). Jacob had a vision, and nothing could hold him back, so Laban told Jacob to set his own salary. Jacob's answer reflected the fact that he not only had physical eyes but spiritual eyes to see what was really going on.

I want my children to know when they leave my house that they have a set of natural eyes to see things with, but more importantly, they have a set of spiritual eyes. They're going to be able to see things others will never see. That gives them a tremendous advantage. No matter where they are, they'll have a vision for the future because the God who made them sees the future and He will show them things to come.

Laban was wheeling and dealing, but Jacob was about to take him to the cleaners because Jacob had already had a vision from God. A few weeks before this, Jacob had had a weird dream about the cows. An angel talked to him and said, "Did you notice anything about your dream?"

"Like what?"

"Well, what's doing all the breeding?"

"Those speckled cows out there."

"Uh, huh. You just might want to remember that."

When Laban said, "What shall I give thee?" all of sudden Jacob thought, "Bingo! We've got a match! I've seen this before." And he knew what to do.

..."Don't give me anything," Jacob replied. "But if you will do this one thing for me, I will go on tending your flocks and watching over them: Let me go through all your flocks today and remove from them every speckled or spotted sheep, every dark-colored lamb and every spotted or speckled goat. They will be my wages."

Genesis 30:31,32

Laban was a thief from the word "go." He cut Jacob's salary ten times. (Gen. 31:7.) Before Jacob showed up, Laban didn't have much because he was a stingy old man.

Don't ever get mad when somebody takes something from you. Don't get mad at your boss. If you think somebody is stealing from you, don't get all worked up about it. If it was legitimately stolen and it was rightfully yours, God's going to not only bring it back, but He's going to bring it back with interest. I don't care if it's been a year or ten years. It will come back with all the interest it's accumulated. Instead of getting bent out of shape because you aren't getting what's due you, trust God to bring it to you with interest. But if you take the offense of it, you won't get to cash that check.

> *"And my honesty will testify for me in the future, whenever you check on the wages you have paid me. Any goat in my possession that is not speckled or spotted, or any lamb that is not dark-colored, will be considered stolen."*
>
> Genesis 30:33

Now watch the wisdom in this. Jacob said, "Here's what I'll do, uncle. I'm going to go through the livestock and keep every animal that is spotted. Whatever is solid-colored, that will be yours." Most of the livestock was solid-colored, so Laban bit into this deal. Jacob said, "If you ever find a solid-colored goat, lamb, or cow in my pen, you'll know I stole it from you."

Laban thought, *That's good. I'll know if he stole it from me.* A thief thinks about stealing all the time. He thinks that because he's stealing from you, you're stealing from him. Laban thought, *I've got myself a stupid son-in-law, and I'll get the contract signed right now.* (v. 34.)

You know what happened. Eventually Jacob moved away with his spotted flocks, which had literally taken over the place. He put three days journey between himself and Laban so he didn't have to worry about Laban messing up anything. And I want you to notice that all through these years with a manipulating, lying employer, Jacob was not only led by vision, but he stayed happy.

Spiritual Vision Keeps You Happy

Spiritual vision will keep you happy.

"Where there is no vision, the people perish: but he that keepeth the law, happy is he."

Proverbs 29:18 KJV

I want happy children. Wouldn't you like to have happy children? The way to have happy children is to help them gain spiritual vision. They will see things others won't see, and no matter who will be messing with them in the natural, they'll know something—and Someone—greater, and it will carry them above trouble.

You can see that in Jacob's life. In Genesis 31:7, he tells Rachel and Leah, "Your father has cheated me by changing my wages ten times. However, God has not allowed him to harm me." How could he say that? How could you work for a company that cuts your salary ten times but say they've not hurt you? It's because God took care of Jacob and showed him a vision to pull him up and over the situation.

Laban was not a good man. Even Rachel and Leah knew that. When God told Jacob to leave Laban, they basically said, "Our own father has cheated us. Let's just get out of here!" (Gen. 31:13-16.) The Bible says, "A good man leaves an inheritance for his children's children" (Prov. 13:22). Laban didn't leave anything for his kids. He was a thief. But because God gave Jacob a vision, he was able to get out of that situation without being cheated or hurt. When you stick with God and the vision He gives you, you'll stay happy and blessed.

How Do You Get a Vision?

You and your children have to have a vision to succeed in life. Here's what I did to develop vision in my family.

The Bible says that before I was born, there was a book in Heaven with my name on it (Ps. 139:16), and it says to write my vision down (Hab. 2:2-3), so I made a notebook for myself, for my wife, and for each of my children. For my book, I took a three-ring binder and put my name on the spine of it. If you pull that book down and open it to the front page, it's all the things about Joe McGee and my life. That notebook has my name in it and what it means. It has a list of my God-given gifts and abilities. It has career aptitude tests I've taken in it to remind me of what my gifts are. It has a written vision of what God has called me to do, and it has the following verses in it:

All the days ordained for me were written in your book before one of them came to be.

Psalm 139:16

"For I know the plans I have for you," declares the Lord, "plans to prosper you and not to harm you, plans to give you hope and a future."

Jeremiah 29:11

"Call to me and I will answer you and tell you great and unsearchable things you do not know."

Jeremiah 33:3

For God's gifts and his call are irrevocable.

Romans 11:29

The secret things belong to the Lord our God, but the things revealed belong to us and to our children forever, that we may follow all the words of this law.

Deuteronomy 29:29

"No eye has seen, no ear has heard, no mind has conceived what God has prepared for those who love him"—but God has revealed it to us by his Spirit.

1 Corinthians 2:9

What does all that do for me? Once I get a vision and write it down, it gives me faith that that vision will manifest in the natural. Faith comes to me when I hear the Word of God. (Rom. 10:17.)

Faith Brings the Vision To Pass

Now faith is the substance of things hoped for, the evidence of things not seen.

Hebrews 11:1 KJV

My faith is always working on what I can't see. So if I'm short on something in my life, it's because I'm short on vision.

Every one of us has faith. Romans 12:3 says that God has given every believer the same measure of faith, which means that the faith we have is quality stuff. Don't ever think you don't have enough faith. Jesus said, "If you have faith like a grain of mustard seed, you can move a mountain." (See Matt. 17:20.) It doesn't take a lot of the faith God gave you to get the job done. You just have to use what you've got!

> *"Whatever things you ask when you pray, believe that you receive them, and you will have them."*
>
> Mark 11:24 NKJV

I have today by my faith whatever I have seen myself doing. Until I see myself doing more, my faith cannot produce more. Faith must have a vision to act upon. My faith is currently producing everything I have seen myself doing, and I can only see what I've asked God to reveal.

What did the woman with the issue of blood see in the natural? She was getting worse. But with her spiritual eyes she saw a Man who healed the sick, raised the dead, walked on water, and fed five thousand, and she said to herself, "If I can touch Him, I've got it" (Matt. 9:21). She had a vision!

When she crawled through the crowd and touched Him, Jesus said, "Woman, your faith has made you whole." Her faith and her vision got her to His feet, where she was healed. She saw it, and her faith brought what she saw to pass.

If we can't see it, we can't have faith to obtain it. Therefore, we cannot have it. Our faith brings the vision God gives us into the here and now.

Seeing the Vision Is Vital

The vision God has planted in us for our lives will continue to get brighter and greater as we walk it out. With every step we take, God shows us more and we gain more.

When He first shows us something, God doesn't dump the whole vision on us at once. He gives us a step at a time so our faith can produce that. Then He'll give us the next step and our faith produces that. This process doesn't end until Jesus comes to get us!

Every person needs vision. That's where the blessing is. If we don't have spiritual vision, we'll perish. The devil and the natural circumstances of life will beat us down. We must have spiritual insight and teach our kids to follow the vision.

People who have made great discoveries are people of vision. Think about Jonas Salk and the Polio vaccine. When others could not see it, he could. Somebody is going to discover a cure for AIDS because they see something nobody else sees. It's going to happen. Somebody saw us on the moon when we weren't even flying off the ground yet.

If all you're seeing is what's there, the devil will keep you depressed. I don't want to be depressed, and I don't want my children to be depressed. I want my children to be happy, so I'm teaching them to have vision.

Self-worth and a vision are two powerful tools to leave home with. With them, we all have a purpose for living, and can feel good about life and about ourselves. Tests and trials may come our way, but we won't stop going forward until we fulfill God's plan.

3

A Love of Math

If kids come out of the home with self-worth and a vision, then they're about to start doing something, and whatever they do is going to produce. That's the will of God.

Jesus said, "I am the vine and my Father is the gardener. He cuts off every branch that doesn't produce fruit, and he prunes the branches that do bear fruit so they will produce even more. You have already been pruned for even greater fruitfulness by the message I have given you. Remain in me, and I will remain in you. For a branch cannot produce fruit if it is severed from the vine, and you cannot be fruitful apart from me. Yes, I am the vine and you are the branches. Those who remain in me, and I in them, will produce much fruit. For apart from me you can do nothing. Anyone who parts from me is thrown away like a useless branch and withers. Such branches are gathered into a pile

*to be burned. But if you stay joined to me and my words
remain in you, you may ask any request you like, and it
will be granted. My true disciples produce much fruit. This
brings great glory to my Father."*

John 15:1-8 NLT

God expects increase in every area of my life. In
3 John 2 we read that God wants us to prosper and be in
health as our soul prospers. In Joshua 1:8 it says if we
meditate in God's Word day and night, then we will
prosper and have good success. Then in Psalm 1:1-3 we
read again that if we meditate on God's Word day and
night that we will live a fruitful life and whatever we do
will prosper. God wants us to be blessed. But that blessing brings with it the responsibility of taking care of what
we are given. God will not give me more of what I do not
take care of. That is why math is so important in life.

*Any enterprise is built by wise planning, becomes strong
through common sense; and profits wonderfully by keeping
abreast of the facts.*

Proverbs 24:3,4 TLB

*For which of you, intending to build a tower, does not sit
down first and count the cost, whether he has enough to
finish it—lest, after he has laid the foundation, and is not*

able to finish, all who see it begin to mock him, saying,
saying, 'This man began to build and was not able to finish.'

Luke 14:28-30

Planning, building, and maintaining the things of life all involve math. How well our kids produce is linked to the third thing no kid should leave home without: a love of math. You see, God is a God of stewardship. Everything God owns is inventoried. From the hairs of our head to the days of our lives, everything is being counted. God is an accounting God who has accounting angels. Reading through the Bible you can see just how important numbers and math are to God. God is a God of great detail. Everything you and I do is being measured and weighed. The Bible says that when we get to heaven we will give an account of every idle word and every deed. (See Matt. 12:36; Luke 16:2; Rom. 14:12; Heb. 13:17; and Rev. 20:12.) If numbers are important to God, and we are made in His image, then numbers should be important to us.

People who know math always seem to have an advantage in life over people who do not. Unfortunately, a lot of kids start confessing early, "I hate math." Most of us started saying it by the time we hit algebra because all our friends warned us about how bad it was. At a lot of schools in

America kids think the algebra teacher is the closest thing to the devil incarnate. (Nobody ever says, "I just *love* my algebra teacher.") Instead, we confess over ourselves, "I hate this class. I'll be glad when I get out of here. How much math do I have to take? I just want the minimum."

Let me tell you something. If you hate math—and most of us have been through that—let me remind you of a little thing that's hooked to math: that's money! Most of the people who liked math in my school are doing really well financially today. But many of the people I ran with who didn't like math are living week to week trying to pay their bills. They don't have any money. They hated math years ago, and they hate math today. Money doesn't stick to them because math and money are the same thing.

The thing that some believers try to do is use their favorite Scriptures to justify not dealing with math and money. Luke 16:13 says, "No servant can serve two masters. Either he will hate the one and love the other, or he will be devoted to the one and despise the other. You cannot serve both God and Money" (Luke 16:13). Then they teach their kids that money is the root of all evil.

The Bible never says that money is the root of all evil. It says that the *love of money* is the root of all evil. (See

1 Tim. 6:10.) That means a person can't truly serve God, giving their whole life and all their possessions to Him, and still remain selfish and greedy, lusting after things all the time. If you really want to serve God, you should serve Him with all your natural abilities and possessions—which includes your money—and your knowledge of math!

God has given everyone the ability to earn a living and to provide for his or her own family. Math is not a worldly, ungodly thing. It was created by God, and He intends for us to use it.

Math and the Economy

Throughout recent years, the United States of America has consistently ranked close to the bottom among the industrialized nations of the world in high school math test scores.

We're a nation that launches space shuttles and builds Mayo Clinics. But what's the deal with us and math? Not only are we usually near the bottom in math test scores, but we're also something else that correlates with our low aptitude in math. We are the number-one debtor nation in the world! We can't control our money; money controls us. Why? We hate math. That explains why most Americans have no working budget.

Americans want jobs so they can make some money, but they hate math. Then, when it comes to tax time we're thinking, *I need to hire somebody to do my taxes. Who knows taxes? Who can understand them?*

If anywhere from 30 to 50 percent of every dollar I make goes to taxes, it might behoove me to know where it's going. I'd sure like to make my money work for me instead of for the government. I believe in the government. I believe we ought to pay taxes. Give Caesar what Caesar is due (Mark 12:17), but don't give him what he's not due! That's crazy!

If I start saying, "I hate math," or "I hate taxes," then I've already shut my brain down. I'm not even trying to think. I've already set myself up. I'm not even trying to get the wisdom of God. But He has so much to tell me. His Word is full of insight into both math and money.

Be sure you know the condition of your flocks, give careful attention to your herds; for riches do not endure forever, and a crown is not secure for all generations. When the hay is removed and new growth appears and the grass from the hills is gathered in, the lambs will provide you with clothing, and the goats with the price of a field. You will have plenty of goats' milk to feed you and your family and to nourish your servant girls.

Proverbs 27:23-27

How can you do business as a shepherd if you don't know how many sheep you've got in your flocks? If you don't know the state of your business—how much you've got in the warehouse or how much capital you've got— how are you going to prosper? Somebody is going to lure you into a business deal, and they're going to take you to the cleaners.

Did you know you have to have a business plan if you have a business? Imagine you're starting up a business and asking for an investment or a loan. What will you say when the investor or loan officer says, "What are you going to do in your business?"

"Well, we're just going to operate."

Not for long! Not if you don't know where you're going with it. You always have to be working on the company you want to have next year, not just on the one you have today. If you don't, you'll be stuck in maintenance mode and you'll never increase.

If we're not willing to steward what we've got, God won't give us any more vision for the future. It's a law of the kingdom. We have to know our financial condition and have a plan for the future in order to increase.

The Bible says, "By wisdom a house is built" (Prov. 24:3). I'm going to give you some Scriptures to get the concrete poured, and then we're going to build something on it.

God Is Big on Numbers

Proverbs 11:1 says, "The Lord abhors dishonest scales, but accurate weights are his delight." This says that God is *delighted* when everything adds up right! We have to have integrity in our financial dealings. I know people are always trying to take advantage of us, but we've got to be honest on our end. We can't control everybody else, but we can control ourselves.

Luke 12:7 says, "Indeed, the very hairs of your head are all numbered." Why would God keep count of the hairs on my head? I don't know, but it must be worth something to Him. I believe this is one of the ways He tells us how much He cares about us and every detail of our lives.

Psalm 90:10 says, "The length of our years is seventy years—or eighty." That's a Scripture where God tells us how long our lives should be. Genesis 6:3 says it could be as many as 120 years. In some places on this planet, a man's average lifespan is much shorter than that. Why does God give us those numbers? So we have something to shoot for. If you don't know the Word, you'll settle for less and think you've lived a long life.

Proverbs 9:11 KJV says, "For by me thy days shall be multiplied, and the years of thy life shall be increased." From the previous Scriptures, I already know that I'm supposed to live to be seventy or eighty, and this verse says God can increase that. That motivates me to stick close to Him and obey His Word!

Order and Math Precede Miracles

God's plan is increase. Faith to faith, glory to glory, brighter and brighter, more and more. Everything God touches increases. Decrease is of the devil; increase is of God. Miraculous increase happens when everything is in order and all the numbers are adding up right.

*For they were about five thousand men. And he said to his
disciples, Make them sit down by fifties in a company.*

Luke 9:14 KJV

If you're going to have a miracle, who cares if the
people are organized or not? Jesus, the Son of God, did.
"Boys, we're going to have to feed 5,000 men and their
families. To do this effectively and efficiently, you'll have
to sit them down in groups of fifty. That way we'll know
if this fifty has been fed or not. If we don't do it this way,
no matter how much food we have, we'll just have mass
chaos out there." For a miracle to happen, they had to
have order.

That's what math is all about: order. Life is numbers.
Did you know that music is math? If you didn't have the
math element, you wouldn't have any melody or harmony.
It would just be chaos. You've got to hit the right combi-
nation of notes at the right time. It's all numbers.

If you're afraid of math, you can't have a miracle. If
you can't count it, then you don't know how many you've
had, how many you've got, or how many you need. God
can't do a miracle for you because you don't know how
much you need.

"We just need some money."

It doesn't work that way.

God doesn't just pull a big lever and say, "Everybody go ahead and grab something." No, He gives a specific amount. If you don't have the vessels, the oil won't pour. (See 2 Kings 4.) Even with the manna in the wilderness, there was just enough for everyone to eat each meal each day. The children of Israel were to collect only a certain amount for each day. If they took more, it would turn to worms and smell.

Sure God moves supernaturally, but He is very ordered and mathematical about it. Everything He spoke into existence is numbered. The stars are numbered. The angels are numbered. The sand is numbered. He has a number for everything. If I mock numbers or order—which is what I'm doing if I mock math—then why would God give me any money to handle? He wouldn't.

I've seen people who didn't seem very spiritual but were very orderly prosper. Somehow they just got to play with more stuff. They got bigger and nicer toys and had them longer than anybody else. Why? It's a law, just like gravity is a law. It's a law of the kingdom that if you steward what you've got and get it in order, you'll bring increase to it. They may not have known God, but they were still functioning according to His principles.

God Keeps a Ledger

In Matthew 25, Jesus tells about a man who owns a huge estate. He was about to leave for an extended period of time, so he called in three of his top overseers and divided the estate among them. To one he gave five parts, to one he gave two parts, and to another he gave one part. Then he said, "Watch over this until I return."

A long time later the master returns and wants an accounting of what he left his servants in charge of. The guy with five talents said, "Master, I've taken the five parts of the estate you left me and I've doubled your holdings."

The master said, "Well done, good and faithful servant. You've been faithful over a few things, and I'm going to make you ruler over a chunk of stuff, because I like people who know how to take care of things and multiply them."

The guy with two parts said, "Master, I got you four parts. I doubled your stuff."

The master said the same thing to him that he said to the first servant, "Well done."

Then the guy with one part said, "Well, I didn't do anything with the part you gave me. I buried it because I was afraid." A lot of people don't want to do any more than they have to do. The world is that way. People will fight you and say, "Man, you'd better slow down. You're working too hard. You'll make the rest of us look bad." I've had that said to me, and my kids have had that said to them. But we can't expect to get more if we don't step out and do more. It's a law of the kingdom.

That last servant said, "I didn't do anything with your stuff. I didn't want to be in charge of it to begin with. I just wanted to punch the clock and be happy. I didn't want to be responsible for any increase. I thought, 'He's left me in charge of this, and if I lose any of it, he'll really get mad. He's a hard man. I know what he does. He's making money where he didn't sow. When he's sleeping he's making money. He's an old stingy guy who likes stuff. I don't want to lose his stuff, so I'll just go bury it so it won't get broken and nobody will steal it out from under my bed.'" (See v. 24.)

The master didn't like that at all, so he said, "The least you could have done was put my holdings into an account so I could have drawn some interest." Then he took his one part from him and gave it to the man with ten parts and said, "Everyone who has will be given more, and he will have an abundance" (v. 29).

Even in the world you hear people say that: "The rich get richer, and the poor get poorer." Well, it's biblical! It's a law of the kingdom, but we haven't understood it.

We know that God's will is that we increase, not decrease, but we haven't been clear on how that increase is supposed to happen. Nobody's going to hand it out to us, and God isn't going to drop money on our front lawn. That's why we have all the Scriptures on work and labor and preparing our fields. It's our job to apply them.

The Bible says that I'm responsible to provide for my family, and if I don't I'm worse than an infidel and I've denied the faith that He gave me. (See 1 Tim. 5:8.) Even infidels provide for their families. We shouldn't be afraid to obey God by stepping out in faith and doing the work He leads us to do. Remember, this is what He delights in! The parable of the talents tells me God is really big on keeping the books straight, and He likes to see the numbers go up.

God expects increase. He expects souls to come into the kingdom. He always wants more. Whatever God Almighty has started, He always finishes stronger. That's a law of His kingdom.

If I'm not good in math, I can't steward what God's given me or get it to increase. In fact, I could even end up working really hard and get less. If I don't deal with numbers and act in faith, I'll end up like the guy with one talent. I'll never increase and God won't be pleased with me.

The Power To Get Wealth

Godly people who love Jesus can end up going to Heaven financially broke. Just because you have knowledge of Jesus doesn't mean you'll automatically prosper. Knowledge of the gospel itself will not produce money. That's only half of the equation. Some people think, *Since I'm saved, say my prayers, and can quote some Scripture, I will be rich.* Yet there they sit broke. I believe the problem has been the lack of understanding of math and how to handle money. We have Bible knowledge of the gospel, but we don't have Bible knowledge of money and math.

Now there cried a certain woman of the wives of the sons of the prophets unto Elisha, saying, Thy servant my husband is dead; and thou knowest that thy servant did fear the Lord: and the creditor is come to take unto him my two sons to be bondmen.

2 Kings 4:1 KJV

In other words, this widow had a husband who loved God and served God but died broke, because he didn't know anything about money. He died and left his family so far in debt that the creditors were coming to take her sons away to be slaves for the rest of their lives to pay off their father's debt.

This is a sad picture of the Church today. We can talk about spiritual things, but we can't go home and run the numbers.

> *But thou shalt remember the Lord thy God: for it is he that giveth thee power to get wealth, that he may establish his covenant which he sware unto thy fathers, as it is this day.*
>
> Deuteronomy 8:18 KJV

God gives us the *power* to get wealth. He doesn't give us *wealth* itself. He gives us the power to get the wealth. That power is in understanding God's order and math.

Are you looking for a financial miracle today? It's really simple. Just start putting some order to your finances. You say, "There's nothing there, Joe." Well, until you find out how deep the hole is, God won't put anything in it.

Think about Moses and the Tabernacle. Do you think he just threw up some goat skins over some poles and said,

"We're going to worship God in there"? No, when God does anything, He's detailed about it. Before the glory showed up to bring supernatural air-conditioning (the cloud by day), heating units (fire by night) (Ex. 13:21), and all the food (manna) they could eat (Ex. 16:15), they had to run the numbers and build it to God's specifications.

God required Israel to let the land rest every seventh year, but they wouldn't run the numbers. They violated the number system for seventy years and didn't let it rest. This was not a suggestion; it was a law, so God said, "If *you* won't let it rest, *I* will *make* it happen." Leviticus 26:35 says, "All the time that it lies desolate, the land will have the rest it did not have during the sabbaths you lived in it." He said, "I'm going to make the land rest seventy times seven years. The numbers are going to balance because an unjust scale is an abomination to Me. There must be order."

The Purpose of Math Classes

Although I never got much higher than a C in high school math classes, at age 28 I decided I'd better start to major in it. Why would I want to spend time on something that I had always done so poorly on in the past?

Because I knew I needed it. In high school, I hated math, and I got what I said out of it: nothing. That's why at age 28 I had to go back and learn what I should have learned in high school. I wasn't interested in math in high school, but now as a husband and father responsible for providing for my family I am very interested in it. I had now learned you only get paid for two things on this planet, what you know and what you can do. I learned I did not know much nor could I do much, and it was time to change. I realized that math was money. The light went on, and I said, "Oh—math equals money and I need some money! I'll take some math!" I got really bold in class and learned to ask questions. "I didn't understand that. Could you repeat that?"

One of the things I tried to do when I taught high school students at the school where I was an administrator was to make the Bible real and practical in every area. I wanted the kids to understand how important math was. I read a wonderful series of books by Ruth Haycock called *Bible Truths in School Subjects*. They were some of the dullest looking books on the outside until you got into them, but they were the greatest set of books ever written for Christian schools. Ruth Haycock took every academic area—algebra, trig, speech, drama, English, foreign language, P.E., health, you name it—and she found every Scripture in the Bible on why we needed to learn it.

As a school administrator I got excited. Before I read her books I would tell my students, "You have to take math because the state says so." But after I got the revelation, I said, "God says you need this to succeed in what He's called you to do." I spent three years teaching that series to my high school students every day, trying to change their attitudes about why each subject was something they needed to know. When we got to the subject of economics—talk about perking up some ears! Every teenager wants cash.

I started out by saying, "Young people, God's will is for you to have some cash. There are some laws about how you get it, and I think the best way to bring this into reality is to find some people on this planet who have a *bunch* of cash."

So we started studying business people, entrepreneurs, and other people who had made a lot of money in their fields. Whether they were businessmen, entertainers, scientists, doctors, or lawyers, we wanted to learn who had money and how they got it.

To go along with the research, each student had to learn what their God-given gift was and find twelve vocations in the world that lined up with it. Then they had a year to interview one individual in each field—a dentist, a lawyer, and so forth—with a specific list of questions that I'd give them. I told them that whatever vocation they'd chosen, they'd find that it takes W-O-R-K to succeed at it.

If they were going to interview a dentist, for example, they needed to find one in the Yellow Pages and set up an interview to speak with them. They'd ask practical questions, such as these:

How much education does it take to become a dentist?

How much money does a dentist make?

What kind of car does a dentist drive?

What kind of house does a dentist live in?

Does a dentist own or lease a building?

When could a dentist retire?

If you could be anything besides a dentist, what would you be?

I had them do this just to make their vision and their faith real. I wanted the kids to see that they were given spiritual gifts, but those gifts were meant to work in the natural realm in very specific ways—ways that would prosper them and bring them blessing.

The Jewish Perspective

In the process of understanding the power to get wealth, I found some interesting things that God told Israel. For example, a Jew could not charge a fellow Jew interest when they loaned him money, but God told them they could charge the Gentiles interest. (Deut. 23:20.) That says that God wants His people to stick together and help each other.

I have always been fascinated with Israel, their history and their modern day culture, because they have always placed a great importance on their children and future generations. There are approximately 14.5 million professing Jews on the whole planet. Almost 48 percent live in America, about 35 percent live in Israel, about 15 percent live in Europe, and the rest are scattered in other countries. Jews make up 2 percent of the population in America,[1] but what an impact they make! And there's a reason. I've heard people spiritualize it and say, "Well, they're God's chosen people." But that's not it! They simply do things according to the Law, which happens to be God's way.

The instruction and education of the next generation is critical to their survival and prosperity, and they give it a high priority in their daily lives.

God had a logical reason for everything He asked them to do. He's not a spooky God who asks people to jump through hoops just for His amusement. God told Abraham in Genesis 18 that He was going to bless him because Abraham would teach his children, his children's children, and all those of his household.

Have you ever met many uneducated Jews? No matter what country they are from, Jewish people usually find a way to become educated—especially about math and economics. It is no coincidence that many Jewish people are prosperous. They think different; therefore, they have different.

How many all-American football players are Jewish that you know of? You probably can't name too many. Yet a large percentage of Nobel Prizes awarded in economics and science have been given to Jewish people.

People have ridiculed them and even complained about their influence, but the fact is that the majority of Jewish people are thriving in this world. I know there are Jews living in impoverished Third World countries, but in the other nations around the world, they are doctors and lawyers, college professors and scientists. Why is that? It's because as a whole, they are well-educated and they are very determined.

Jewish people are very determined because they have to be. They can't remember a time when they have not been persecuted. It didn't begin and end in 70 AD when the Temple was destroyed. It wasn't just in Germany during the Holocaust, when millions of Jews were killed. They have been persecuted and hunted down all throughout history.

From 1908 to 1922, a man by the name of Julius Rosenwald, the son of a Jewish immigrant, served as president of Sears and Roebuck. Before his death in 1932, the private foundation he started financed the building of over five thousand schools in the South to help fight racial prejudice. He spent millions of dollars of his own money to do it.[3]

A lot of Jews are not just prosperous, but they're also extremely benevolent. They don't like to see injustice, bigotry, or prejudice, and they give money to organizations that fight those things because they have been victims of those things for centuries.

All of this goes back to their childhood and how they were raised. I don't care if they were poor, making bread in the back of a sweatshop in New York City. As a whole, Jewish children understand from birth, "You're going to make a major impact. You're going to make a mark in society." And they do.

Three Things Jewish Children Are Taught

In all the things I've studied about them, it seems to be universal that Jews are taught three things as children. First, they learn that they are valuable. Most Jewish children learn about their family tree and their heritage. They develop a pride and inner strength from knowing their ancestry and history.

Second, Jewish children learn to defer their gratification. Their parents don't give them everything the moment they ask for it. They might say, "You know, I can get you some cheap toys now, but if we can defer this and save, you can go to a fine school and make a lot of money." You know, the longer you wait to get your toys, the more expensive those toys that you're going to get will be.

Third, Jewish children learn that knowledge is worth money. Their parents tell them, "The most valuable thing you possess is knowledge because it's mobile. You can take it with you. You can lose everything you've got, move halfway across the world, and get your life back because you have knowledge."

These three things will profit anyone of any race or culture.

The Wisdom of Math

In the Book of Joel God says to Israel, "Since you've repented, your wheat bins and vats are going to overflow. You're going to increase. You're going to be full. You're going to be satisfied. All these blessings are going to come on you." (See Joel 2:19-27.) Then He says, "And afterward, I will pour out my Spirit on all people" (v. 28). When I saw this, I thought, *If you know how to handle money, you get to handle spiritual things. There's a pattern there.*

So if you have not been trustworthy in handling worldly wealth, who will trust you with true riches?

Luke 16:11

Prospering in the spiritual and prospering in the natural are connected. We need to teach our kids that whatever they work at in life, God expects them to increase and prosper. Hopefully they will love what they do and will do what He tells them. But they also ought to know how much they're being paid, how much is being deducted for taxes, and how much they can save and invest. We need to teach them that doing this pleases God. It is spiritual!

I don't want my children to leave home and have no concept of how money works. I don't want them always griping because they haven't got money or whining because they're afraid they won't ever get any. I want them to settle the issue before they leave home that math is one key they need to be successful. If they know something about math, then they can get money. They don't have to become mathematicians or teach in a college, but they can learn how to run the numbers. Anybody can add and subtract.

God said that as long as the Earth exists, there would be seedtime and harvest. (Gen. 8:22.) Somebody will be making money, and God said it's supposed to be us! Our money puts people in heaven. You might not know them in this lifetime, but your money will put them there. But if we just have an "us-four-and-no-more" mentality, we won't have any extra to give.

God's Word says, "I'll give you wisdom if you don't have any." (See James 1:5.) By the time our kids leave home, they should believe that He'll give them the wisdom they need in the area of money and that His increase will follow. Our kids can go out and change the world when they have a love for math and know God's purpose for money.

1. I have self-worth because I know that God loves me.

2. God has a purpose and vision for my life. I am here for a reason.

3. I must use math to plan, budget, and monitor the progress of that vision.

4

Organizational Skills and Time Management

The fourth thing no child should leave home without is something that thousands of grown men and women will go to a seminar and pay big bucks to learn about: organizational skills and time management. This is a struggle for many people, and there is a reason why. Daniel 7:25 says that the antichrist's system is constantly working on the world to bring *disorder.* The devil is the author of confusion. God does everything decently and in order. He designed this world with order, but the devil wants to mess that up.

Because of the world, the flesh, and the devil, we constantly fight disorder. The Earth is having birth pains trying to throw off the sin that's on it. Sin brings disorder, chaos, fighting, and wars. The world's system (which runs on sin and disorder) and God's kingdom (which runs on righteousness and order) are at war with one another. (Rom. 8:7.)

The Bible says that we live in this world, but we're not of this world. We belong to the kingdom of God, so this world is not our home. Someday we'll go home to Heaven, but while we're here we've got a job to do. To live as members of another world—the kingdom of God—we must think differently than everyone around us thinks. We live on this planet as ambassadors, pilgrims, and strangers. And if we're going to *thrive* here, we'll have to get organized and take control of our time.

Organization Never Stops

Getting organized isn't something you do just one time. It isn't like you say, "I got organized the third month of my ninth-grade year, and I've been organized ever since." That doesn't happen. You're always organizing.

Recently I heard an interview with one of the astronauts who went to the moon in 1969. He said that even after years of planning and calculating, on the way to the moon they had to do a course correction every fifteen minutes. Their whole trip was one long series of adjust-ments. One time they were fourteen degrees off course after just fifteen minutes! At fourteen degrees off, they would have missed the moon like a barn door.

Because you're always going to be organizing, the first step to bringing order to your life is to get past the frus-tration. Life is a constant series of amending, adjusting, and repairing. There are things you can't see, even after all your planning and praying, that will try to mess up your schedule. Don't get depressed that you have to continu-ally reorganize, straighten, and reorder. That's just part of living on Planet Earth.

Bringing order to things is part of what we do as chil-dren of God. The world's system brings disorder, but we're from God, who does everything decently and in order. Wherever we show up, we bring God's order onto the scene. That's why we have this rule at my house: "Don't ever leave a room without leaving it better than you found it, no matter who was in there before you were there." That's part of teaching our kids to take responsibility, becoming responsible for things that aren't even your fault.

I remember catching one of our kids coming out of the bathroom and saying, "Whoa, go in there and pick up your towel."

"That's not my towel."

"I don't care whose towel it is. You know the rule of the house. Pick it up. You leave that room better than you found it."

That rule will almost keep your kids out of the kitchen. I've caught them coming out of the kitchen, and I'd say, "Whoa, what's that on the counter?"

"That's not mine."

"It is now!"

You know that if you don't have a mentality like this, your house will look like the city dump in about three hours. Chaos will hit, which brings discouragement and depression. When depression comes, efficiency goes out the window. When you're depressed, you don't get anything done. All you want to do is take a nap, thinking, *Maybe someone will come and clean it up while I'm asleep.* It's not going to happen! It takes constant work to bring order to things and to maintain it, but we can't get all worked up about it.

Order maintains an environment of energy, creativity, and productivity. When you develop organizational skills early in life, you have an advantage over everybody else, because when you live in order, you live in peace. We need to teach our kids that order brings peace, and when they have peace it is a lot easier to hear from God, to know what to do, and to get His strength to do it—no matter what life and circumstances throw at them. That's being led by the Spirit.

Being Led by the Spirit

It seems someone or something is always messing with our plans and schedules. Even Jesus had to deal with it. Jesus had an appointment to heal Jairus's sick daughter. He was on his way there, right on time, when along came this woman who grabbed Him by the coattail and spun Him around. Jesus didn't say, "Woman, you don't understand. I've got an important engagement. Somebody is dying, and I can't deal with you now." Instead He stopped in His tracks and took care of her. He didn't get frustrated because He had peace. His life was in order.

After the woman was healed, the devil didn't stop trying. He kept messing with Jesus. He showed up after that and said, "You're too late. You messed up your schedule. You missed your appointment. The girl is dead."

But Jesus said, "No, she's not dead. She's just sleeping." That's because He was always in command. It might have looked like He wasn't, but He was. The Spirit of God knew exactly what was happening, and Jesus' every step was directed and sure because He was led by the Spirit.

For as many as are led by the Spirit of God, they are the sons of God.

Romans 8:14

I honestly believe that you can teach your children to be led by the Spirit. You can put this wisdom inside their hearts before they leave home. I've told my kids, "The world will always try to mess with your schedule. Don't be upset by that. You'll always have to adjust and let the Holy Spirit lead you. He'll tell you how to navigate the situations you didn't anticipate."

Life can overwhelm us at times, and we have to turn to God for wisdom and strength when the curve balls come at us or we will lie down and quit. But when we keep things in order on the inside, we'll have the ability to keep things in order on the outside. We'll become more efficient and be able to handle more responsibility. And most important, we'll get to help more people.

First Corinthians 14:40 NKJV says, "Let all things be done decently and in order." In this Scripture, Paul was writing to the Church about the miraculous gifts of the Spirit flowing. Before the Holy Spirit can manifest in a supernatural way, we must have order.

Titus 1:5 KJV says, "For this cause left I thee in Crete, that thou shouldest set in order the things that are wanting." Paul essentially said, "Titus, you know, the people got saved, but it's a mess over there. The reason I sent you there was to put that place in order so that the Holy Spirit can move and the church can grow and mature."

> To every thing there is a season, and a time to every purpose under the heaven: He hath made every thing beautiful in his time.
>
> Ecclesiastes 3:1, 11 KJV

God knows the times and the seasons. If our kids learn how to be led by His Spirit, they will always come out on top no matter what they go through in life.

God Will Help You Get Organized

Order is a thing we will always deal with because we're in a world that has no order. Weather patterns are messed up. The economy *seems* messed up. Nothing seems to be stable. The only stability on this planet is the wisdom of the Word of God. The wisdom and knowledge in us will be the stability of our times. (See Isa. 33:6.)

> *So teach us to number our days, that we may apply our hearts unto wisdom.*
>
> Psalm 90:12 KJV

We need God's wisdom to teach us to use the days He's given us. We can pray, "Lord, I need You to teach me how to organize my day."

God said, "I know what you need before you ask, but you need to ask." (See Matt. 6:8-9.)

We need to teach our kids to let the Lord order their days–to let the Holy Spirit show them what to do, when to do it, and how to do it. Do you know why most students do poorly in school? It's not because they're stupid or because they have low IQs. Most of the time it's because they're disorganized!

As a school administrator, I'd say, "Do you know why your grades are down?"

They'd say, "Well, I lost my homework." "I forgot the assignment." "I showed up late." "I didn't have my book." It wasn't that they couldn't do well academically. It's that they were disorganized.

Did you know that nobody was born organized? Babies are born naked—not organized! We have to *learn* how to be organized.

The Problem With Keys

There are so many things we need help with. For example, wouldn't it be wonderful to go look for your car keys and know where they are? In my immediate family, we now have eight people driving. I'm telling you, we used to have keys everywhere! Not only were people losing their keys, but then people started swapping. They'd say, "Oh, you don't have your key? Take mine." *Well, there's the beginning of chaos to the max!*

I'd come home and see one of my kids standing outside the house in the rain. I'd ask, "Where's your door key?"

"I don't have a key. I gave it to Sarah."

"What did she do with it?"

"She gave it to Jessica."

And Jessica would say, "Well, I think I left it at school."

After awhile I didn't have any window screens on the bottom floor of my house. My children broke every screen so they could open the windows to crawl into the house. Our neighbors must have thought we were the weirdest bunch of people. I just know they were saying, "What's the matter with those people? They're always crawling in the window. Why don't they use the door?!" I'll tell you why we didn't use the door—because nobody could ever find their keys!

At first I thought, *This is the devil! We've got to bind him!* But then I realized that we just had to get organized. We finally came up with a system that worked, and we haven't had that trouble again. Now we've all got colored key rings with everybody's name on them. I said, "You're blue, you're green, and you're yellow." Sometimes I'd have to say, "You don't have yellow keys. Those aren't yours! *Put 'em down!*"

We also keep spare sets of keys in other places. We glue extra keys under the cars. And now we have something in our kitchen that doesn't look very pretty, but it's very efficient. We put up huge hooks. I don't mean little, dinky ones. I put big, brass coat hooks up, and everybody has their own. When my kids come in, their keys better go on their hooks! It's been a long time since anybody went without a set of keys.

Until we got our keys organized, though, we were always yelling at each other. You know how it is. It's because of the pressure. We're late to go somewhere—work, school, the airport—and we can't find our car keys. When we finally got where we were going, someone would ask, "Why were you late?"

There we were, grown people, saying, "I lost my keys."

Thank God people wouldn't ask, "How did you lose your keys?"

If they did, we'd have to hang our heads and say, "I'm disorganized."

We fixed that problem by getting organized!

Hair Trouble

We used to have trouble with hairbrushes too. Nobody could ever find a hairbrush. I'd think, *How do we have six women in the house and not one of them has a hairbrush? I've got a hairbrush, and I don't even have that much hair!*

The problem got so bad that I finally had to fix it. I bought those stretchy cords and fastened them to the wall in the bathroom with toggle bolts and wire. Now all the hairbrushes just hang on the wall. We also bought hair dryers like they have in hotels. They stay fastened to the wall. You don't have to worry about losing your hair dryer, taking it off to school, leaving it in the locker room, or leaving it on the bus on some field trip. Where's the hair dryer now? *It's screwed to the wall!* We eliminated that problem by getting organized.

Then we had to address hairspray. (Six women in the house, remember.) We started buying hairspray by the gallon, and we probably had three dozen of those little plastic spray bottles. If you ran out of hairspray, there were four or five gallons in the pantry. You could just fill up your bottle again.

There are some things we're still working on. Shoes are a problem. We've tried bins and hangers on the door, but you can only put so many pairs of shoes on them before they break. But that's okay. We're not upset. We're like the astronauts going to the moon. We just keep making adjustments as we go along. The world is a world of disorder, but we're determined to bring order to our lives because we want to live in peace.

People who have order have more peace. They get more done. They're more efficient. They wake up ready to do something. If you wake up with dishes piled up in the sink and clothes scattered everywhere and nothing to wear, you start thinking, "Dear Lord, I don't want to do anything or go anywhere." But if you get up and you're already organized, you have some pep in your step. You're saying, "Let's get after it."

Commit thy works unto the Lord, and thy thoughts shall be established.

Proverbs 16:3 KJV

A man's heart deviseth his way: but the Lord directeth his steps.

Proverbs 16:9 KJV

The steps of a good man are ordered by the Lord: and he delighteth in his way.

Psalm 37:23

Notice that you have to have some plans, and to get some plans you're going to have to pray. God knows we need help. He tells us, "I made you, and I'll help you" (Isa. 44:2). He helps us, and then we help our kids.

Teaching Kids Organization

There's really only one way to help kids get organized, and it's not by yelling at them. You have to literally *train* them and walk them through it. I wish there were an easy way, but there's not.

In our home my wife is the anchor of our organizational efforts. She's the one who makes everything happen. She'd go through all the backpacks and pocketbooks every evening. It was like a ritual, and she had it down to a fine art. That's how she knew what was going on.

I used to think, *Isn't that an invasion of privacy?* But it wasn't. It's just one of the requirements of living in my house. If you're a kid in our home, it's an unwritten rule that Mama owns you. Until you own yourself, you are hers.

We have day planners for all our kids. Two of my kids use them religiously. They're very orderly. Their papers are all in their notebooks with tabs and notes. But then we still have another kid who's already grown whose notebook looks like a circus has come to town and three tornados have landed in the middle of it.

I ask, "How could you get so disorganized from this morning to tonight? Did you get in a wreck? Did you shake your bag upside down?"

"No."

I've learned that it just takes longer for some people to get it than others. Some people will finally get frustrated enough to reach out for help, and then they'll catch on.

One of the things I suggested when I was on a Christian school accreditation team was a mandatory class to teach students organizational skills at about the sixth-grade level. Organizational skills and time management have to become a habit. Unfortunately, a lot of school administrators said, "We don't have time. We've got to cover math, science, and English. We don't have time for an organizational class."

I'd say, "If you don't get your students organized, those academic classes won't amount to much of anything in their lives. But if you get them organized, they can take the world by storm."

These skills have to become part of your life. You can't get them from a speech or a weekend seminar. You have to make them a habit every day. Some days you'll hate doing it, but if you don't you'll always be behind, and that will pay you back some bad interest.

Time Management

The biggest reason why people don't organize their lives is that they think they don't have time for it. I know I've been guilty here. I've said, "I don't have enough time." But that's really not true. I have as much time as anybody else does. I just need to find out how to get a hold of it.

Benjamin Franklin said, "Does thou love life? Then do not squander time; for that's the stuff life is made of."

I'm going to tell you how to get a handle on your time. What you need to do is get a little pad of paper or a notebook and, for three days, write down *everything* you do and how long it takes you to do it.

I know what you're thinking. I can almost hear you say, "Dear Lord, I don't have time!" But if you don't do this, you'll *never* have time. So, starting tomorrow morning and continuing for three days, write down everything you do. Your notebook entries may look something like this:

Woke up 6:15 A.M.

Showered, shaved, got dressed 6:35 A.M.

Toast and coffee 6:40 A.M.

In the car 6:45 A.M.

At work 7:10 A.M.

Make a note of everything you do for all your waking moments. If you go to the bathroom, drink a cup of coffee, talk to a friend, or talk on the phone, you need to write it down. If you do that for three days, I promise you'll find some time. We all waste time, but we just don't know it because we can't see it.

Sleep

We all get twenty-four hours a day, and most human beings spend one-third of that time sleeping. If God designed us to spend that much time sleeping, sleep must be important. Therefore, to be organized and efficient your sleeping time is critical. That means *where* you sleep is very important.

I don't know why, but for some reason we don't place much importance on our beds, even though we spend one-third of our lives on them! If we're going to be efficient and effective, we need to put some thought, prayer, and money into our sleeping areas. Your sleeping area ought to be like a temple. It's not where you store boxes, extra file cabinets, clothes, or anything else. It's where you go to spend one-third of your time so you can be effective with the other two-thirds of your time.

You ought to be sleeping on the best mattress. You ought to have nice pillows under your head. You ought to have a good, working clock. In fact, get two or three clocks so you don't have to worry about whether you'll wake up on time. I have three clocks in my bedroom, one manual and two electric. When I lie down I don't worry about oversleeping.

The bedroom is the last room that most people put money into, is it not? It's where we go and pass out from all the other stuff we've been putting time and money into, but it's usually a mess. Then we wonder why we wake up sore. We think it's because we're wearing ourselves out doing other stuff, but if we'd do something with our bedrooms and take sleep seriously we'd wake up refreshed and be able to do more.

You may not feel like you have the money to improve your bedroom, but this is a faith thing. You're going to have to start believing God. It took my wife and me six months to believe God for our bedroom furniture. It was one of our big prayer projects. The old bed we had was propped up with two-by-fours. We couldn't move a certain way, or it would collapse. We slept nervously. We were thinking all night, *Don't turn over.*

Maybe the reason the bedroom is the last room we put money into is because nobody sees it. We put money into the stuff other people see, like the living room and dining room. When visitors come we just shout, "Close the bedroom door!" But if God set it up so that we would rest one-third of our time, it must be important to Him, so it should be important to us. We need to be rested up to do what we're doing for God.

Teach your kids the importance of sleep by putting some time and effort into their bedrooms too. Don't run out and buy something cheap. Put it on a prayer list and start believing God for the money to buy some good quality furniture. Our kids shouldn't be sleeping with toys, dirty shoes, and video games piled all over their beds with three dogs wrapped around their feet. We need to clear those things off and get our children used to sleeping in an orderly place. Otherwise, they'll wake up frustrated. They'll grow up feeling confused because there's no order in their lives.

Use Only One Time Management System

Once we get their sleeping areas organized, we need to teach our kids how to best use the time they have when they're awake. To begin, we need to get something for them to write their schedules in. Some people like Day-Timers, Franklin Planners, or different computer programs. It doesn't matter what you use; just use something. I once heard that Lee Iacocca never used a day planner. He used a yellow steno pad. Every night he'd write, "Here's what I have to do tomorrow" at the top of a page along with everything he needed to get done. Then he'd spend the next day scratching off what he accomplished. If he didn't get something done, it moved to the next day on his yellow pad. His method was so simple, and it worked.

Whatever your kids use, have them use just one thing. Nobody should be using three calendars. If you do, you're just playing with your mind. Get one system, and stick to it.

What To Write

You need to teach your kids what to write in their daily planners.

1. They should write the things they have to do. These are fixed things that are locked in. For example, school starts at approximately 8:20 A.M. That's not an option. Then they should write down what time English, history, math, and their other classes are. Next have them write down their other fixed commitments for the day, such as basketball practice or play rehearsal.

2. They should schedule essential daily activities, including eating and sleeping. They're going to eat three times a day, and they're going to sleep every night. Now, most of us—and especially kids—underestimate the need to schedule sleep. However, if we don't write down what time we're going to go to sleep, we won't go to sleep when we're supposed to. Whatever time they have to be at school the next day is not flexible, so they need to write down when they should be in bed to get enough sleep for the night.

They'll say, "I'm not sleepy." That doesn't matter.

Say, "Get into a horizontal position on your bed and read until you are. Drink a glass of warm milk. Find some way to get your body to sleep!"

Young people are notorious for staying up until 1:00, 2:00, or 3:00 A.M. and waking up cranky and moody. Eventually it's no different than the land that Israel wouldn't allow to rest. God said, "Enough's enough. You're out of here, and I'll make the land rest." You can only go so long without getting eight hours of sleep. I know some people say they can make it on five. There are a few who can, but they're the exceptions.

Have your kids write down what time they'll go to sleep and what time they'll get up. They need to have a fixed time to get out of bed. They shouldn't let it just float around. They need to establish a good habit of getting quality rest.

3. Your kids need to schedule review times. Here's where a lot of us miss it with academics. I tell young people that the best times to review a subject are when they first get out of a class or when they get home from school. It's said that what we learn will stick about 80 percent better if we review it right after we've heard it. If your kids will just do this every day, they'll have an

advantage over every other student who's cramming till midnight while watching TV, listening to CDs, eating a cheeseburger, and trying to visit with their friends on the phone. If your children can take twenty minutes right after the class to review what they learned, while it's still fresh and the momentum is still rolling, it will be more effective than three hours late that night.

4. They need to schedule recreation time. If they don't block it off, it will take up all their time. I know it did mine when I was growing up. I loved to play football. After ball practice, some of us guys would shower, get back into our street clothes, and walk back out on the field to throw the ball for another two hours. We ought to have been at home, but we wanted to stay and play some more ball. Every waking moment, we were playing ball.

Unfortunately, playing ball is not something I do for a living today, so all that time didn't produce a whole lot. I had a great time, but it didn't produce anything for me for today. That's why recreation time should be clearly scheduled.

5. Your kids need to schedule preparation time. This is something we have to *make* our kids do. Preparation time is spent developing skills that they will use in their careers. They need to ask themselves what they're going to do and then plan to develop the skills for that. This may mean going to basketball camp to prepare for the upcoming season or to develop their skills so they will improve by the next season. It might be taking courses that teach them how to take the college entrance exams so that when they sit down to take the SAT or ACT they know what to expect and how to do well.

Learning how to prepare for the road ahead is a skill your kids will always use because whatever field they eventually work in, it is not going to stand still. Everything in the world is changing, and your kids need to be able to change with it.

The 80/20 Rule

There is an important rule that every person needs to know about scheduling their time. It's called the *Pareto principle* also, but it's more commonly known as the 80/20 rule. This principle developed by Italian economist

Vilfredo Pareto in 1906 states that for many phenomena, 80% of the effects come from 20% of the causes. In other words, this rule helps us to get the most important things done first. It prioritizes all the things we have to do. The devil will try to pressure us into doing things that are less important when our time gets tight, so the 80/20 rule helps us to keep from falling for the devil's distractions.

Let's say you have ten things to do in a day, but you don't ever get all ten things done. Something's always coming up, and by the time you crawl into bed, you've only gotten half of one thing done. Here's how the 80/20 rule applies: If I have ten items on my to-do list one day, two of those items probably carry 80 percent of the value of my list. What's really important to me is usually tied up in just two of those ten things. The other eight are important, but they're not nearly as important as those two. Each day I need to figure out which two of those ten things are going to provide the most benefit and get those two done first. If I don't get the other things done that day, it won't devastate or destroy me. If I'm pressed for time, I don't need to get bogged down with the things on my list that aren't as important.

Prioritizing Commitments

Once your kids start writing these things down, they'll realize they don't have a whole lot of spare time left. The time they actually have to manage is really short. They don't have twenty-four hours to manage because most of their twenty-four hours is already booked. The part that's left to manage is really quite small—which makes it very valuable.

That's why we need to prioritize our commitments. For example, I fly almost every weekend for my ministry. I'm traveling forty-eight or fifty weeks a year, so I lose about fifty days a year just sitting on airplanes. Therefore, I catch a lot of early morning flights. Why? Because I want to get home. I'd rather be kissing Mama, eating a cheeseburger, or doing something that's productive at home—not sitting in an airport.

I have people ask, "When's your flight, Brother Joe?"

"It's at 5:50 A.M."

"In the morning?"

"Yeah. See, you're here with your wife. I'm going home to be with mine."

I want to be with my family. I know it's hard on some people to get up and take me to the airport before the sun comes up, but if I don't get control of my time, the devil will steal it. I'll end up being nice to everybody except the people who are the most important to me.

Everyone's situation is unique, but the devil will mess with your time if you don't have priorities and a plan. You don't want to be rude. If someone asks, "Hey, do you have time for this?" you can look in your Day-Timer and say, "No, I'm sorry. I have something planned." If you don't have a plan, the devil will keep people—usually nice people—in your face to make plans for you. You can always be flexible and be led by the Spirit, but you always want to have a plan.

You Can Do It!

You can do this, and your kids can too. When kids don't organize their lives and manage their time, they'll be the slowest in the class. They'll have the worst grades. They'll be the ones the teacher doesn't like. They'll think everybody is against them. But when they learn to organize their lives and manage their time, they'll be the best and the brightest. They'll know where they're going and how they're going to get there, and they'll have the time to do what they want to do.

The most important thing about being organized is to do what you can and trust God for the rest. Don't get frustrated when you have to keep putting things in order. Jesus didn't get frustrated and say, "I thought I just healed a bunch of sick people. What are all these other sick people doing here?" He understood that the world is chaotic.

Organization and time management are skills that we all must learn, and we have to seek God for His direction in these areas every day. If we don't organize our lives and schedule our time wisely somebody else will do it for us—usually the devil!

The devil's always trying to paint a vision that says, "You don't have time to do that." God has a different vision, and we have to get hooked up it. He'll teach us to number our days, to order our steps, and to manage our time so we can get it all done. Make sure your children learn this before they leave home.

5

A Teachable Spirit

But the meek shall inherit the earth; and shall delight themselves in the abundance of peace.

Psalm 37:11 KJV

In the Sermon on the Mount Jesus quoted that verse saying, "Blessed *are* the meek: for they shall inherit the earth" (Matt. 5:5 KJV). In other words, the meek will inherit this world's stuff. We always think of a meek person as being wimpy and weak, and some people think, *Well, if I'm just quiet and shy, God will promote me.* But that's a lie. You won't find that anywhere in the Bible. To be meek means that you're teachable. It means that you're humble and you're not full of pride.

If you're teachable, you'll inherit the Earth. Why? Because if I walk into a room and want to prove to you how much I know by doing all the talking, I won't learn anything. But if I'm willing to walk into a room and be humble, if I'm willing to learn and gain knowledge by asking questions, God will exalt me because I've submitted myself to Him and to those around me. I've humbled myself and put myself in a position to receive.

If I'm learning all the time, I'll know more and I'll get to do more. Who wrote most of the New Testament? It was one of the most educated men of his time, the Apostle Paul. That's not a coincidence. Paul was always learning and teaching what he had learned to others. And when he was imprisoned he wrote as the Holy Spirit moved him, giving generations after him the Word of God. Even when he was about to be executed, Paul asked Timothy to bring him "the books, but especially the parchments" (2 Tim. 4:13 KJV). He was reading, studying, and writing right up to the very end of his life.

You see, it's all about stewardship. Paul was a great steward of everything God showed him. God will give me stuff according to my ability to handle it. If I increase my ability, I will get to handle more. It's like the order part of math. If I get things in order, I get more stuff. It's not whether God likes me or doesn't like me. God loves me. That issue is settled, but the spiritual law is that I don't get any more of what I can't handle. That law works whether I'm smiling or not, whether the sun's shining or not, and whether I'm happy or sad. Spiritual laws work all the time. Increase comes when we prepare for it.

Pride Prevents Learning

According to God's Word, people who are teachable are humble, and God will exalt them. It should be our goal as parents to train our kids to be teachable, especially by the Lord.

> *And all your [spiritual] children shall be disciples [taught by the Lord and obedient to His will], and great shall be the peace and undisturbed composure of your children.*
>
> Isaiah 54:13 AMP

> *The fear of the Lord is the beginning of wisdom; all who follow his precepts have good understanding. To him belongs eternal praise.*
>
> Psalm 111:10 KJV

Being reverent and having a healthy respect and awe for the Lord is important because it keeps us teachable in all situations. That kind of humility enables our kids to gain knowledge and wisdom from the Lord, and that will bring them great peace in the midst of turmoil.

I've seen people who drag their heels and refuse to learn new concepts or new technologies. Sometimes older people say, "I've never needed it before, and I don't need it now. I'm too old to be learning that stuff." If we think that way, we'll get left behind. We always need to be learning new things. Did you know that the majority of all new jobs today are independent contract jobs? The average American changes vocations—not jobs, but *vocations*—five times in his or her lifetime. That means five times in life, our kids are probably going to have to learn something totally, absolutely brand new.

If they're unteachable, proud, arrogant, and bitter they'll be left on the side of the road while life blows right by them. The Bible says, "The wicked flee when no one pursues, but the righteous are bold as a lion" (Prov. 28:1 NKJV). We need to be bold enough to try new things and to learn new concepts.

The world says, "You can't teach an old dog new tricks," but that's not true. The Bible says we have the ability to learn new things. The Holy Ghost will be our teacher and show us things to come. (John 16:13.)

Why are people afraid of learning something new? Somebody might say, "I don't want to look stupid." I'll tell you what looks stupid: it's when we're so proud and arrogant that we won't learn! Proverbs 6:16-17 says there are seven things that God hates, and one of them is a proud and haughty spirit. That's the person who thinks, *You ain't teaching me nothin'. I don't want to know what you know. I already know everything I need to know.*

> *Pride goes before destruction, a haughty spirit before a fall.*
>
> Proverbs 16:18

Not only does God hate the person who thinks they know everything, but arrogance and being unteachable cause a lot of misery and failure in life. We should never go into a new situation trying to impress everybody with what we know. We should be humble and teachable. We need to go in asking questions.

Humble People Ask Questions

We need to teach our children when they're young to ask questions and not to brag about what they've done. They need to get busy and learn what they're supposed to be learning.

Whosoever therefore shall humble himself as this little child, the same is greatest in the kingdom of heaven.

Matthew 18:4 KJV

What is a child like? I've seen lots of little kids, and they're not what we think of as humble. They're loud and rowdy, and they ask a bazillion questions. "Why?" "Why?" "Why?" "Why?" "Why?"

I've got six kids, and they must have asked me millions of questions down through the years. But as they've grown I've taught them to ask *important* questions, questions whose answers will unlock the future for them and enable them to serve God with excellence.

Another characteristic about children is that they watch and copy each other. We call it peer pressure. There's a good and a bad kind of peer pressure, but the good kind is really good because we can learn a lot from each other.

I'm a traveling minister, and I love to see what other traveling ministers are doing. Many know things I don't know. I want to read their newsletters and see how they do meetings so that I can become more efficient and effective at what I do. I want to learn what they know because there are families all over this planet fussing and fighting with each other, and I've got the answer. It's a simple answer, but I have to get to them with the Word of God. It's my responsibility to get the Word to them, so I'm constantly looking for ways to reach out with the message God has given me.

You do not have because you do not ask.

James 4:2 NKJV

People get saved because they ask questions. God says, "You want to get to Heaven? Ask a lot of questions. Ask. Seek. Knock. You've got to ask." (See Matt. 7:7,8.) It's a legal situation with Heaven. If you're not willing to ask, you can't get anything. You've got to be humble yourself like a little kid and ask questions.

"God, can You give me salvation?

"God, can You give me Jesus?"

"God, can You give me the Holy Spirit?"

"God, can You give me wisdom?"

"God, can You give me direction?"

"God, can You give me peace?"

If you don't ask for it, you won't get it.

If you want to, you can get arrogant and say, *I won't ask for anything.*

Do you know why won't men ask for directions? It's because we don't want to look stupid. "I don't need directions. I don't need help. I can get us out of here." But you're still lost! That old sin nature is hard and stubborn. You have not because you ask not!

Humility Versus Pride

James 4:10 says, "Humble yourselves in the sight of the Lord, and he shall lift you up." God doesn't want us to be humble so He can squash us. He wants us to be humble so He can lift us up.

Some teachings have painted the mental picture in Christians that being meek is the same thing as being weak. But that's not what God says: "If you'll ask, I'll give you the power to get wealth. I'll give you power over the devil. I'll give you power to be a witness. I'm not going to do everything for you, but I'll give you the power to do it yourselves." (See Deut. 8:18; Mark 3:15; Acts 1:8.) If we're meek it means we're willing to receive from God, and He will exalt us.

How do we get lifted up? By doing what God showed us to do. How can He show us what to do? We just need to humble ourselves and ask Him. He'll lift us up by giving us revelation, understanding, wisdom, courage, and strength. But if we're unteachable, we'll fail.

My people are destroyed for lack of knowledge.

Hosea 4:6 KJV

Have you ever had to deal with an arrogant kid who thinks he knows everything? That's a bad way to grow up. If he's proud and unteachable he won't learn or grow or reach his potential in life. Kids who won't be taught will have destroyed lives. That's why we need to help them be teachable. It's an act of love to train our kids to have good study habits and to learn from their teachers in life.

Study to shew thyself approved unto God, a workman that needeth not to be ashamed, rightly dividing the word of truth.

2 Timothy 2:15 KJV

If you're studying, listening, and being teachable, you won't be ashamed. On the other hand, if you're trying to prove how smart you are, you're going to fall flat on your face. God makes it simple. Pride will destroy your life, but humility will bring you blessing and peace.

God Will Help Us To Get What We Need

If our goal is to be humble and teachable, where do we look for the knowledge we need? There's a ton of information out there, so how do we weed out what we need from what the enemy's trying to throw at us? I believe the Spirit of God will lead us to the right information. He'll direct me to the right people, the right places, and the right books I need to read to find the information I'm lacking.

Without question, though, the most important book of information I can pick up is the Word of God. It has the knowledge and wisdom I need for every area of my life. It's the foundation for everything else I learn. Every bit of information I encounter either agrees with or opposes the Word of God. Therefore, I believe you have to wash your mind daily with the water of the Word or you'll be deceived. One of the best ways I have found to wash myself with the Word is to write Scriptures down on three-by-five note cards and confess them over myself regularly. I have four main areas in my life that I need God's help in, so I have a stack of cards for each one.

1. Organization

The first area I need help in is organization, so every day I ask God to help me be organized. I confess by faith that I am organized. Why? Because by nature, I am not an organized person. I have the following Scriptures written down.

> So teach us to number our days, that we may apply our hearts unto wisdom.
>
> Psalm 90:12 KJV

> The steps of a good man are ordered by the Lord: and he delighteth in his way.
>
> Psalm 37:23 KJV

> For God is not the author of confusion, but of peace, as in all churches of the saints.
>
> 1 Corinthians 14:33 KJV

> Let all things be done decently and in order.
>
> 1 Corinthians 14:40 KJV

> Commit thy works unto the Lord, and thy thoughts shall be established.
>
> Proverbs 16:3 KJV

I put my face up to the mirror in the morning and say these Scriptures over myself. "God, I thank You that I'm an organized person. My family's organized. My ministry is organized. We've got it together because of You." You'll start to think differently just talking to yourself like that!

2. Efficiency

The second area that I need help with is efficiency, so I humble myself daily and ask God to help me be more efficient. It takes work, and I need God's help, so I confess Isaiah 40:31 KJV over myself.

> But they that wait upon the Lord shall renew their strength; they shall mount up with wings as eagles; they shall run, and not be weary; and they shall walk, and not faint.

When I'm tempted to say, "I don't want to clean out the garage," or "I don't want to balance the checkbook," I humble myself and say, "No, I'll run and not get weary. I'll walk and not faint."

> I guide you in the way of wisdom and lead you along straight paths. When you walk, your steps will not be hampered; when you run, you will not stumble.

> Proverbs 4:11,12

When I lean on God's ability and wisdom, I believe I'll have the endurance I need to be efficient and productive. My steps will not be hampered, and I will not stumble.

Maybe sometimes you're afraid to start a project because you don't know how deep it's going to get. You know how that happens. You start to clean out the garage, and what you thought was a thirty-minute project ends up taking three days! You think, *I never should have started this.* But that's all right. With God's help you'll not grow weary. You'll get it done, and it'll make you sleep well.

Isaiah 40:4 says,

Every valley shall be raised up, every mountain and hill made low; the rough ground shall become level, the rugged places a plain.

God will smooth out your plans. You just need to ask Him to do it. "Lord, I've got a lot of stuff to do. Can You give me some help?" He helped Israel when all they did was repent. (vs. 2.) He made the high places low and the low places high. He can do the same for you so you can run and not stumble or fall on your face.

My confession is this: "I'm getting twice as much done in half the time. God said He'd teach me to number my days, and He does things exceeding, abundantly, above and beyond all I could ever ask or imagine. So I believe, according to the Word of God, that I get twice as much done in half the time."

3. Finishing

The third area that I need help with is finishing what I start, so I humble myself daily and ask God to help me be a finisher. Finishing what we start is vital to everything we do in life.

Take, for example, the Bic pen. The guy who invented the Bic pen is not the guy who marketed it. A guy from Hungary designed it, but it kept leaking on him, and he never patented it. A guy from France who designed the ink for it so it wouldn't clot or run finished it and patented it. His name was Marcel Bich, and he shortened the name of the pen to Bic.[1] The Panama Canal is another example of someone not finishing. The French first started the construction on it, but they kept running into problems and finally gave up. The United States finally solved those problems and finished the Canal, so we're the ones who got the credit for building it.

God says, "I am the Author and the Finisher of your faith. What I began in you I will complete." (See Heb. 12:2.) He wants me to finish what I start. God says, "Son, what I have asked you to do is something that needs to be done, and I will finish it. You either get to do it, or I'll get somebody else to do it, but this will be finished."

A lot of people make it in life not because they started something, but because they picked up something somebody else dropped and finished it. I don't want anybody finishing for me. I don't want to spend my whole life working on something, then fall down in front of the finish line and have somebody else finish for me and get the credit. The Apostle Paul felt the same way. He said, "If only I may finish the race and complete the task the Lord Jesus has given me—the task of testifying to the gospel of God's grace." (See Acts 20:24.) Paul knew how important it was to finish what he had started.

> "Suppose one of you wants to build a tower. Will he not first sit down and estimate the cost to see if he has enough money to complete it? For if he lays the foundation and is not able to finish it, everyone who sees it will ridicule him, saying, 'This fellow began to build and was not able to finish.'"
>
> Luke 14:28-30

I don't want somebody making fun of me. Jesus wants us to think about what we're committing our lives to. He wants us to count the cost and to finish what we start.

One man who was instrumental in getting me into the ministry is not in the ministry today because he couldn't finish. Things got tough and he quit. I'm not going to lie to you: sometimes it can get tough. We can let circumstances get us down, but we have to look to the Author and Finisher of our faith. God says, "My grace will be sufficient. Whatever is coming against you, I'll get you through it." I choose to believe that even though others have chosen not to.

Some things in life are hard, but we have an inside track through Jesus Christ. We need to take ownership of the calling we've been given. When it gets tough, we need to see it as opportunity—not just as opposition. Then we can say at the end of our lives, "I have fought the good fight, I have finished the race, I have kept the faith" (2 Tim. 4:7).

Up in Heaven, we'll be probably be asking one another, "Did you finish?"

If we've remained humble and teachable, we'll be able to say, "Yeah, I did it. I finished."

Even Jesus said, "I finished. I got it done!" In John 17:4 KJV, He says, "I have glorified thee on the earth: I have finished the work which thou gavest me to do." We can do that too. We can glorify Him and finish our work with His strength and wisdom. On the other hand, we can finish in a way that doesn't bring glory to Him.

James 1:15 says, "Then when lust hath conceived, it bringeth forth sin: and sin, when it is finished, bringeth forth death." That's a bad finish. Selfish lust leads to sin, which leads to death. That is not the way we want our lives to go, so we need to stay teachable. Then we will finish what He's called us to do.

4. Endurance

The fourth area that I need help with is endurance, so I humble myself daily and ask God to help me endure. I stand on Ephesians 6:18, which says, "And pray in the Spirit on all occasions with all kinds of prayers and requests. With this in mind, be alert and always keep on praying for all the saints." This Scripture speaks of the importance of persistence and consistency.

When life is difficult, we need endurance. We need to say, "I'm not quitting. I'm going to win—and I'm going to win big. I'm not getting out of the race. I don't care what I see. I'm not quitting."

My stack of three-by-five cards on endurance includes these Scriptures:

Endure hardship with us like a good soldier of Christ Jesus. No one serving as a soldier gets involved in civilian affairs—he wants to please his commanding officer.

2 Timothy 2:3,4

Weeping may endure for a night, but joy cometh in the morning.

Psalm 30:5 KJV

But you, keep your head in all situations, endure hardship, do the work of an evangelist, discharge all the duties of your ministry.

2 Timothy 4:5

Paul told Timothy, "Get your job done. God's given you favor, grace, peace, strength, joy, and guidance. Endure, and get it done."

Endure hardship as discipline; God is treating you as sons. For what son is not disciplined by his father?

Hebrews 12:7

As you know, we consider blessed those who have persevered. You have heard of Job's perseverance and have seen what the Lord finally brought about. The Lord is full of compassion and mercy.

James 5:11

At the end of his life, Job had double what he began with. It happened because he endured and kept his heart right toward God.

Keep Learning

People who leave home with a love of learning will go places in life. That's because nothing stands still in this world. If we're not willing to increase our learning, we're going to get left behind. No matter how good we are at something today, we won't be that good at it three months from now. Somebody else will be better.

The Bible says that the world is ever learning, but they're never able to come to the knowledge of the truth. (2 Tim. 3:7.) But that's not us. If we'll let Him, the Holy Spirit will give us witty inventions and show us things to come. We can stay ahead of the game.

Don't ever say, "I can't learn that." You have the mind of Christ! You can learn anything you want to learn. You can learn a foreign language. You can learn a whole new vocation. If you'll humble yourself, God will exalt you by giving you what you need to do the job. That means you're going to learn. If you want His wisdom, you're going to sit down at His feet and ask a lot of questions.

Everything I have, everything I own, everything I have accomplished is a result of doing everything I currently know. If I ever hope to have more than I currently have or do more than I am currently doing, I will need to learn more than I currently know. I must stay teachable.

> *If any of you lack wisdom, let him ask of God, that giveth to all men liberally, and upbraideth not; and it shall be given him.*
>
> James 1:5 KJV

When you train your kids to have a teachable spirit, they will become who God has created them to be. Then they'll be ready to share the things God has taught them—and for that they'll need the sixth thing that no kid should leave home without.

6

Communication Skills

People who have the ability to communicate effectively go far in life. I've seen it in school, I've seen it in ministry, and I've seen it in work. We have to teach our kids how to communicate.

People can think a thousand different things when they hear the words *communication skills*, but usually it is not what the Bible says. In the world people who have the gift of gab have an advantage over people who don't. Now that doesn't mean that they know anything. Their mouths may be yapping while their heads are empty. As we say in ministry, "Anybody can draw a crowd, but it takes somebody with some knowledge to hold them there."

When we talk about communication skills, we need to go deep. You need to get past the surface because whatever comes out of your mouth is going to be a direct result of what's inside of you. Working on your technical speaking skills will not help anything if you just open your mouth and stick your foot in it.

Nobody cares how technical I get if my heart is hard. I can say all the right words and enunciate clearly, but if my heart is messed up my words won't do anybody any good.

Communication Comes From the Heart

For out of the abundance of the heart the mouth speaketh. A good man out of the good treasure of the heart bringeth forth good things: and an evil man out of the evil treasure bringeth forth evil things.

Matthew 12:34,35 KJV

If you're going to work on your communication skills, the first thing you have to work on is your heart. You need to be filling your heart with good things. The best thing you can put in your heart is the Word of God.

Let the word of Christ dwell in you richly as you teach and admonish one another with all wisdom, and as you sing

*psalms, hymns and spiritual songs with gratitude in your
hearts to God.*

Colossians 3:16

*Finally, brothers, whatever is true, whatever is noble,
whatever is right, whatever is pure, whatever is lovely,
whatever is admirable—if anything is excellent or praise-
worthy—think about such things.*

Philippians 4:8

*Speak to one another with psalms, hymns and spiritual
songs. Sing and make music in your heart to the Lord,
always giving thanks to God the Father for everything, in
the name of our Lord Jesus Christ.*

Ephesians 5:19,20

What's in our hearts will roll out of our mouths
whether we want it to or not. That's why Proverbs 4:23
says, "Keep thy heart with all diligence; for out of it are
the issues of life." If I talk to you long enough, whatever
I'm worried or excited about will come out because what's
in my heart comes out of my mouth. It's a law.

If I want to be a good communicator, I have to learn
to guard my heart and only put good things in it. I can't
be a great conversationalist unless I've been filling my
heart with something worthwhile.

What You Say Gives You Away

I can talk to people and know in a few moments if they've ever read a newspaper. I know if they read any periodicals. I know if they know about business. I know if they've read any good books lately. If they're talking about what they did in junior high, I can tell they haven't learned much since then. It doesn't take long to find out what a person fills himself up with.

You can get around someone and find out pretty quickly if they're able to carry on a conversation, because once you get past the weather and "How are you doing?" it slows down.

I don't care what you do for a living. You ought to be able to carry on a conversation about something. But you can't communicate with people if you don't have anything inside of you. That doesn't mean you have to fill yourself up with the things of the world. It just means that you ought to be able to carry on an intelligent conversation.

Most of us are like, "What's up?"

"I don't know. What's up with you?"

"I don't know. There's not much to me."

"See you later."

"All right."

We didn't even hit the water on that one, let alone go deep.

As parents, we need to help our kids gain knowledge in specific areas so that they can build their communication skills. We need to help them acquire good taste in three things. I realize these things may not sound very spiritual, but each one will help your kids develop good communication skills.

1. A Love of Good Books

We need to help our kids develop a love for learning, and that's going to start with books. God created humans to read and write. A giraffe can't read and write. A zebra can't read and write. As much as I love my dog, even he can't read and write. Only humans can read and write.

God knew we were going to need to do a lot of reading and writing in order to pass on the knowledge we have. That way it can go places we're not. A lot of the books I read were written by people who may have been dead for years. They're gone, but their knowledge and understanding is still here because they left it in print. Maybe the person who wrote the instruction manual to your car is not alive anymore, but thank God he left you the book on how to fix it before he left. If nobody ever wrote anything down, we'd have to reinvent and rediscover things every day.

To develop a love for good books in your children, you have start reading to them when they're little. There's no shortcut. But once they gain that love, they will always be learning something that they can pass along.

2. A Love of Good Music

The second communication builder kids need is a love for good music. Music is powerful. I love all kinds of music, but I love some kinds more than others because of where I was raised and my personal tastes. If you let me get control of that radio dial, it's going somewhere that my wife or kids wouldn't ever take it.

I can hardly spell the word "classical," but I love classical music. Classical music relaxes me. I can work when it's playing. I love listening to that stuff. I also love good bluegrass music. We've got some great Christian artists out today who are producing great music, and my family can go to boot-scootin' on those songs. We can dance all over the living room floor and wear the wood out.

I love a little country. I like a little jazz. I love a lot of the oldies. I love Nat King Cole, and I've got everything he ever sang. I love Dean Martin's and Perry Como's stuff.

Maybe you're asking, "Who in the world is that?" Well, I'm older, but the important thing is that I love music that you can listen to and understand. I love songs about loving your wife and your kids, about having a dream for something. I don't want to listen to songs that make me wonder, *What are they talking about?*

If we want our kids to have good taste in music, we have to teach them about it. We can't just yell, "Turn that racket off!"

They'll ask, "Why?"

"Because I don't like it."

No, that won't work. The sin nature will rebel at that. What we have to do is educate our kids. It's like leading a cow to the barn. You can *drive* a cow into the barn—in which case she'll kick you and leave you something to step in. Or you can get in front of her and *lead* her into the barn—in which case she'll love you and let you milk her. Then everybody will be happy.

If we want our kids to appreciate good music, we have to get out in front of them and teach them about it. I've taken my children to some strange places. We've been to Branson, Missouri, and heard every bluegrass and country singer you could imagine. We've been to the Tulsa Performing Arts Center and heard classical and pops orchestras. We've listened to some great modern stuff too.

I've exposed my kids to different musical styles and asked them during concerts, "What do you think about that?" They tell me what they think, and I don't give an opinion. I just make observations. "Have you ever seen that instrument before? You just thought there were guitars and drums, didn't you? Check that out."

Often they begin to develop a taste for what I've exposed them to. I tell them, "Music is wonderful. God made music. You're going to hear a ton of it in Heaven. Every time we get together, we're supposed to have some. You ought to have some in your house, in your car, in your garage, and at your work."

Music is powerful, and I want my children to love and appreciate it. But if I don't teach them about it, they'll gravitate to whatever comes around.

That's what we did when Elvis came along. We said, "Dad, that was good."

"What was he saying?"

"I don't know, but watch him move. Woo-hooo!" The music wasn't hitting our head; it was just hitting our flesh.

We need to teach our kids to use their brains and their hearts when they choose music. Music is a language of its own. It's always communicating something. We need to instruct our kids to be discerning about it. Not only will this help them build their communication skills by giving them something intelligent to talk about, it will help them to watch what they put into their hearts.

3. A Love for Good Food

The third thing we need to help our children develop a love for is good food.

"Food? Joe, I thought you were talking about communication skills."

I am. The reason developing this is so important is that so much of the time, conversation takes place over a meal. I've seen kids completely shut down their opportunity to communicate because somebody set some dish in front of them and they curled up their noses at it. They just blew their opportunity to fellowship.

In days gone by, I've taken my own kids to a relative's house, a restaurant with a visiting minister, or another person's home, and all of a sudden they stopped the conversation dead in its tracks because someone put something other than their normal macaroni and cheese in front of them. They've made faces and groaned.

I've told them, "If you ever do that again, as soon as I get you outside, I'm going to buy a gallon of that and you're going to eat it. You're going to learn to like a lot of foods. And if you don't like it, you've learned one thing not to ever eat again. But you're always going to try it the first time and be polite."

We eat a lot of first-time foods at my house. I'll say, "Check this out."

"What is it?"

"It's the first time."

When I say that, they know, *Uh oh, the first time— gotta smile and gotta like it.* And they do a good job at it. They try it and say, "Mmm, great."

The Bible says in Acts 2:42 that the church grows in four ways: doctrine, fellowship, breaking of bread, and prayer. One of the four ways the church will grow is by eating together. The Bible also says that all believers ought to be given to a spirit of hospitality. (Rom. 12:13.) Hospitality usually involves serving a meal. Our kids ought to know something about food other than just how to nuke a hot dog. It will give them an advantage in their ability to communicate effectively in all kinds of different settings.

Conversation Rules From the Word

The Bible is a great reference book for improving conversation skills. I'm going to give you some rules for conversation skills that come right out of the Scriptures.

1. Speak Slowly

We have to learn how to speak slowly and softly. How are we going to win the world for Jesus when we don't know how to talk to people?

Wherefore, my beloved brethren, let every man be swift to hear, slow to speak, slow to wrath.

James 1:19 KJV

We're supposed to be slow to speak. How do you react when somebody's talking ninety miles a minute and you can't get a word in edgewise? You probably don't like that very much.

2. Speak Softly

Loud people don't make you feel good. Did you ever have a kid come into your house and just yell, or have somebody greet you hollering? Your body releases those fight-or-flight hormones, and it just feels terrible. You want to say, "Calm down a little bit."

> A soft answer turneth away wrath: but grievous words stir up anger.
>
> Proverbs 15:1 KJV

> If a man loudly blesses his neighbor early in the morning, it will be taken as a curse.
>
> Proverbs 27:14

In romantic movies, have you ever heard the hero yell, "HEY, HOW ARE YOU DOING, SUGAR?!" That won't get you any kissing. A soft word works much better.

> The woman Folly is loud; she is undisciplined and without knowledge.
>
> Proverbs 9:13

We want to be disciplined and knowledgeable, not loud and foolish. Loud people who run their mouths all the time won't make any friends.

3. Avoid Offensive Words

Proverbs 11:22 says, "Like a gold ring in a pig's snout is a beautiful woman who shows no discretion." Denise and I were on a plane a while ago, and a very attractive, well-dressed couple in their mid-forties got on. They had their Calvin Kleins on, her makeup was just right, and he was tanned. They just looked like an upper-middle-class, yuppie couple—until she opened her mouth. I never heard more curse words come out of a woman in all my life! She thought it was so funny. She wasn't mad. She was just holding a conversation. Oblivious to anyone around, she couldn't get eight words out without throwing a cuss word in there. She was pretty, but I thought, *I've got a dog I'd rather be around than you.* It was repulsive.

Then I wondered, *How did he get stuck with her?* Until he opened his mouth.

He looked like a nice businessman, but when he started talking, I thought, *Man, you've got an IQ of about four and a half. You got yourself all dressed up looking nice, but you're full of dead stuff.*

I don't know how they got to be that way, but evidently they had no friends because a real friend would have gotten in their faces over their behavior by now.

They needed someone to tell them, "You need to tone this down and get some substance in your heart so that something pleasant comes out of your mouths." They needed some iron-sharpening-iron friends. (Prov. 27:17.) They never even guessed that they were offending so many people around them.

Have you ever known a person who couldn't talk without starting a fight? That's what the Bible calls a fool. "It is to a man's honor to avoid strife, but every fool is quick to quarrel" (Prov. 20:3). I've been a fool before. Thank God we can all repent and learn to grow up!

If any man offend not in word, the same is a perfect man, and able also to bridle the whole body.

James 3:2 KJV

That would be good if we could go through life without offending anybody with our mouths! Unfortunately, we're prone to sin, but thank God we can repent and apologize.

The best way to avoid offensive words is to speak very few words and to think before we speak.

When words are many, sin is not absent, but he who holds his tongue is wise.

Proverbs 10:19

The heart of the righteous studieth to answer: but the mouth of the wicked poureth out evil things.

Proverbs 15:28

Proverbs 29:11 KJV says, "A fool uttereth all his mind: but a wise man keepeth it in till afterwards." I love a good conversation, but you don't have to tell your whole life's story. Don't tell *anybody* your whole life's story...unless they ask you for it...repeatedly!

Ephesians 4:29 says, "Do not let any unwholesome talk come out of your mouths, but only what is helpful for building others up according to their needs, that it may benefit those who listen." Boy, there's one for a plaque. If you're not going to bless somebody, don't uncork!

Acquiring Conversation Skills

I'm going to give you four practical points for developing conversation skills. You should pass these things on to your children.

1. Look for Common Ground

When you don't know how to begin a conversation with someone, look for something you have in common with them. Where are you standing at the time? It could be in an elevator on a college campus or at work. You could say, "Are you new here?" or "Are you coming or going?" Just find some common ground to start a conversation.

2. Don't Do All the Talking

This is a biggie. I'll discuss this point in more depth later in the chapter.

3. Ask Questions

You can keep the conversation alive by asking questions. This is the greatest advice about developing communication skills. The best way to be a great conversationalist is to ask the other person questions. You'll learn something and the other person gets to tell you about himself or herself. People feel good about themselves when you ask them questions, and they love you for it. It's a good way to make new friends.

One thing to remember, though: make sure that you ask the right kinds of questions. Don't ask inappropriate things, such as, "How much money do you make?" or "How's your sex life?" I've seen grown men ask some of the craziest things. Apparently their brains were empty, and that's all that was rolling around in there.

4. Be a Good Listener

When someone else is talking, be a good listener. Good listeners have some distinct characteristics. First, *they don't interrupt when someone else is speaking.* Practice this with your spouse and children. We're always more likely to let down our guard and get sloppy with those we are the closest to.

Second, *good listeners pay attention when someone else is talking.* This is a good one. Your spouse asks, "Are you listening to me?"

And you say, "Why would you ask that?"

"Because you're staring out the window. *Are you listening to me?*"

Give your full attention to what the other person is saying, and look them in the eye when they're talking.

Third, *good listeners respond to the feelings of the speaker.* If someone's crying about something, don't start laughing. If they're laughing about something, don't start crying. Respond appropriately to the emotion that they're communicating.

Fourth, *good listeners comment on what the speaker has just said.* I always try to repeat what someone tells me.

That helps me with two things. Number one: once I say it, it's locked into my memory. I remember what I say more than what I hear. Number two: repeating what they say tells them, "I heard you." It lets them know that I was really listening.

Scriptural Principles of Conversation

Now that we've seen some practical, natural principles of conversation, I want to give you four basic principles from the Bible.

1. Don't Talk Too Much

Ecclesiastes 5:3 KJV says, "A fool's voice is known by a multitude of words." If you talk too much, you'll end up saying something you'll regret. I know. I've done it. I've walked away from somebody and thought, *What in the world was I talking about? What did I say that for? We had a great conversation for an hour, and then in the sixty-first minute, I went brain-dead and said something I had no business saying.*

You're talking to somebody and getting that relationship going, and all of a sudden you share something with them that they had no business knowing. They didn't need to know, but you went and told them. You're knocking your head against a wall, saying, "Oh, I shouldn't have told them that. I promised somebody I wouldn't repeat that. But I was running short on words, and, hey, the tank was going dry." You've been there too, haven't you?

2. Don't Talk About Yourself All the Time

Philippians 2:4 KJV says, "Look not every man on his own things, but every man also on the things of others." If you're talking, don't talk about yourself all the time. "I," "I was," "I did," "I'm going to," "I wish." You get the picture.

How about, "What do you do?" "What do you think?" "How did you do this?" "What are you planning?" Think on another person's things, not on your own. It'll make you some friends.

3. Don't Brag

Don't toot your own horn. Proverbs 27:2 KJV says, "Let another man praise thee, and not thine own mouth; a stranger, and not thine own lips." It's a really simple rule: Let other people brag on you; don't brag on yourself.

4. Don't Exclude Other People

First Peter 3:8 KJV says, "Finally, be ye all of one mind, having compassion one of another, love as brethren, be pitiful, be courteous." Have compassion and be courteous. Don't exclude a third party from your conversation.

I get opportunities to practice this rule all the time. After a church service or a meeting, I can get caught up in a conversation with somebody and see somebody else standing there in my periphery. They're not a part of my conversation, but they're still standing there. At that point I have an opportunity. I can just keep laser-locked on the person I'm talking to and think, *I hope that other person will go away.* Or I can look at them while I'm talking to the first person and include them in the conversation. I don't do this when we're talking about personal things, but I do it whenever we're having a general conversation.

You've been excluded before and it doesn't feel good, does it? You're standing there when someone is talking, and they're acting like you're not even alive. That's not being very courteous, and it's not a good crop to reap back a hundredfold!

Diseases of the Tongue

The Bible also talks about several problems that we can have in communication. These are what I call diseases of the tongue.

1. Excessive Talking

This is what I talk to teenagers the most about. If you want to be a great conversationalist, don't talk too much!

God is in heaven, and thou upon earth: therefore let thy words be few.

Ecclesiastes 5:2 KJV

God's in Heaven, and you're here. No matter how much you know, next to God you don't know much, so don't say much.

The wise in heart accept commands, but a chattering fool comes to ruin.

Proverbs 10:8

People are thinking, *Man, that guy won't shut up.* That's not good, is it?

People who are always talking are usually restless people.

But no man can tame the tongue. It is a restless evil, full of deadly poison.

James 3:8 KJV

If you're nervous and concerned, you just can't shut your mouth down. That's the result of a restless heart.

Some people talk for the sake of talking because they can't stand it if it gets too quiet.

2. Idle or Careless Words

But I tell you that men will have to give account on the day of judgment for every careless word they have spoken.

Matthew 12:36

I don't want to have to settle those accounts. "Lord, forgive me for my careless words, and put a guard on my mouth!"

Simply let your 'Yes' be 'Yes,' and your 'No,' 'No'; anything beyond this comes from the evil one.

Matthew 5:37

When we're talking, we need to think about what we're going to say and not just babble our whole brain. A wise person will consider what they are going to say before they say it.

3. Gossip

There are lots of good Scriptures on this one.

Do not go about spreading slander among your people.

Leviticus 19:16

A gossip betrays a confidence; so avoid a man who talks too much.

Proverbs 20:19

The words of a gossip are like choice morsels; they go down to a man's inmost parts.

Proverbs 18:8

Everybody loves gossip. Somebody asks, "Hey, did you hear about Sister So-and-So?"

"No, tell me more." It's like chocolate-covered cherries or a banana split. It goes down good, but then it kind of makes you nauseated after a while.

What are you going to do with that information? You can't pass it on. That's a sin. You're like a garbage can that can't be picked up, so maggots start to form. *There's a mental picture of gossip to keep in your mind!*

Lord, who shall dwell [temporarily] in Your tabernacle? Who shall dwell [permanently] on Your holy hill? He who walks and lives uprightly and blamelessly, who works rightness and justice and speaks and thinks the truth in his heart, He who does not slander with his tongue, nor does evil to his friend, nor takes up a reproach against his neighbor.

Psalm 15:1-3 AMP

Do you know what taking up a reproach is? That's to let somebody talk to you about something you know isn't good. The Bible says not to take it. That's tough, because it means you have to risk offending another person. But if you take up a reproach by listening to gossip, you'll be included in the deal.

If I listen to gossip, my friend can say to someone else later, "Yeah, I was talking to Joe the other day, and we just feel that...." If the lid went open on my garbage can and I took it in, I'm now a party to it.

When I was a school administrator, I had a rule that I would not entertain *any* complaints about a member of my staff. A parent would come in and say, "Mr. McGee, I want to talk to you about one of your teachers."

I'd say, "Really? Did you talk to them yet?"

"Nope, don't want to."

"Then I'm not talking to you. That would be a violation of Scripture. In Matthew 18:15-17 Jesus says that if you've got an offense against someone, you have to go to them first. After that, if you are still having problems, I'll be more than happy to talk to you. I'll be your second, but I won't be your first."

If I hadn't done this, the parents would be able to go to my staff member—whom I hired and love and am trying to encourage—and they'd say, "We were talking with Mr. McGee about you, and we're going to do something about this." Then I'd be the bad guy. I'd be the garbage man again.

My staff knew I wouldn't listen to any complaints about them. I'd send the complainer to the staff member first. After that they could come to me. This not only demonstrated my loyalty to my staff, but it also set the godly standard of dealing with offenses the way the Bible tells us to deal with them.

4. Lying

The Scriptures are packed with references to this disease of the tongue.

> *There are six things the Lord hates, seven that are detestable to him: haughty eyes, a lying tongue, hands that shed innocent blood, a heart that devises wicked schemes, feet that are quick to rush into evil, a false witness who pours out lies and a man who stirs up dissension among brothers.*
>
> Proverbs 6:16-19

You ought to memorize these seven things the Lord hates. I've got them on a note card labeled "DON'T DO

THESE!" Notice that the second thing of the seven things the Lord hates is a lying tongue. Proverbs 12:22 says, "The Lord detests lying lips, but he delights in men who are truthful." Jesus said,

> *You belong to your father, the devil, and you want to carry out your father's desire. He was a murderer from the beginning, not holding to the truth, for there is no truth in him. When he lies, he speaks his native language, for he is a liar and the father of lies.*
>
> John 8:44

When the devil lies, he speaks his native language! If he's your daddy, you're talking his language, which is lying. I don't want the devil to be my daddy. I got rid of him, and I want to speak my new native language: the truth.

Liars don't have a promising future. Revelation 21:8 says, "But the cowardly, the unbelieving, the vile, the murderers, the sexually immoral, those who practice magic arts, the idolaters and all liars—their place will be in the fiery lake of burning sulfur. This is the second death." Notice it says *all* liars.

I don't care how long you and I have been walking with Jesus. Telling a lie is the easiest thing we've ever done. It just rolls right off our lips. Lightning doesn't strike us. She-bears don't rip our flesh off, so we think,

That was pretty easy. No, we just stuck a bad seed in the ground, and when it comes up it's going to get ugly. We'd better rip that thing out quickly and get rid of it because the disease of lying is a destructive force.

5. Hastiness of Speech

This is simply talking before you think. It's not considering what you say before you say it.

> *Seest thou a man that is hasty in his words? There is more hope of a fool than of him.*
>
> Proverbs 29:20

Remember Moses in the wilderness? Instead of speaking to the rock as God instructed him, he struck it with his rod. (Num. 20:9-12; Ps. 106:32,33.) He lost his temper, didn't think, and it kept him from going into the Promised Land.

The righteous don't make haste. (Isa. 28:16.) Every time I feel like I'm in a real hurry, I know that's not God because the righteous don't make haste. There's no time in Heaven, and God knows exactly what being on time on the Earth means, so the devil is the one who's pushing and driving me to do something stupid. When I'm late for something and I'm under pressure, my mouth uncorks and here it comes!

We all need to slow down and think before we speak. If we'd slow down our mouths and let our hearts and minds engage first, we'd say what we should—no more, no less.

Practice Communicating

Communication skills are important. Go buy yourself a great book on etiquette because every one I've ever read has a chapter on communication skills. If you'll take what you learn there and practice the biblical principles listed in this chapter, you'll become a great conversationalist.

Some people just seem to be born with great conversation skills, and as a result, they have tremendous advantages in the workplace. But even if you aren't a natural communicator, if you'll practice using the principles in this chapter, and if you'll share them with your kids, you and your family will be on the path to great success in life because you'll be speaking with the wisdom of God. Then when you add the next thing we'll be talking about, you'll be able to share His wisdom not only in words but also in deeds.

7

Character

The seventh thing that no kid should leave home without is such an important thing. As parents, we can instill it in our kids, especially when we have the Scriptures to turn to. This vital quality is character. I don't mean a part that you act out in a play. I'm talking about character of the heart.

The Scriptures themselves are the best resource for building our kids' character.

Train up a child in the way he should go: and when he is old, he will not depart from it.

Proverbs 22:6 KJV

And, ye fathers, provoke not your children to wrath: but bring them up in the nurture and admonition of the Lord.

Ephesians 6:4 KJV

Doing what's right is not a decision. It's a habit that you learn. You start with a decision, but then it becomes a habit. That's why you need parents and people in authority over you. We wouldn't do right if there weren't people in authority in our lives.

If there wasn't a boss, you wouldn't show up on time.

"When do you show up?"

"When I get ready to get there."

I've seen this happen, especially in ministry. It just seems like the ministry is a little more lax sometimes. When we're doing a TV production, for example, the schedule starts at 7:00 A.M. If Billy Bob is not there on time, we're paying people big money to just wait around for him to show up. We've got high-dollar camera people doing nothing, the lights are burning, and the makeup lady is waiting. Everybody's there except Billy Bob, who doesn't realize he's costing us money because no one taught him character. He is not respectful of others' time. I like what I heard one boss say: "If you're on time, you're late!"

Character is vital to your kids' success in life.

Daniel, A Young Man of Character

Daniel served under three heathen kings, and it was said of him, "We perceive in this man an excellent spirit." (See Dan. 6:3.) What they saw was his character, and his character was developed in his home.

When Daniel was just a teenager he was taken captive by a pagan army and brought to a foreign land as a slave. The character Daniel had developed at home caused him to thrive there. He had no problem learning the Chaldean customs, language, or religion because he had already been trained in the ways of God. He learned about them, but the Chaldean gods meant nothing to him because He knew the one true God.

Daniel's first big challenge came with the Chaldean food. He had been brought up to eat only certain foods in Israel. Mom and Dad had told him, "You can't eat such-and-such kind of food—ever." But in captivity, Mom and Dad weren't there. Daniel was probably upset because he had been ripped away from his home and country, and someone set a big plate of the heathen king's food right in front of him. It looked good. It smelled good. It was a high-dollar smorgasbord. But it was the food his parents taught him never to eat.

Daniel was a teenager in a foreign land. What do teenagers do when they're away from home? They eat what they want to eat. I know I did. I went traveling when I was a teenager, and I ate everything. I said, "Put it all on there, and put some ketchup on it!"

Daniel was thinking, *I don't want to mess up. I'm already in a strange land. They might chop my head off if I don't eat this.* He was looking at a big feast, but he said, "I've got to do what I've been taught and what I know is right. I can't eat this." Daniel had character; he had integrity.

The server said, "You've got to do it, or I'll lose my head."

"No," Daniel said, "just feed me and my Hebrew friends vegetables for ten days. If we don't look any better, fine. But trust me: we'll be all right." (Dan. 1:8-13.)

After ten days Daniel and his buddies were found to be healthier and wiser than anybody else in the palace. (v. 15.) Because Daniel had integrity and character, he could stand up and do the right thing—no matter who was watching or what kind of pressure there was.

Remember Proverbs 29:18 KJV says, "Where there is no vision, the people perish: but he that keepeth the law, happy is he." Do you want happy children? Children who do right are happy; children who do wrong are unhappy.

God said to Cain, "Cain, why aren't you happy? It's because you're not doing what's right. If you were doing right, you'd be happy." (See Gen. 4:6-7.)

The way to be happy in life is to do what's right no matter who's watching. We're happy when we're not feeling guilty. When we're doing what's right, we don't have trouble sleeping. When we've got clear consciences, we're happy campers!

Character-Building Qualities

If we want to experience consistent happiness, we have to be people of consistent character. If we want our kids to be happy, we need to give them opportunities to build their character. There are several qualities we need to teach our children to help them develop character.

Obedience

Children who are taught to obey become people of character. Character building doesn't allow many exceptions to the rule of obedience. Children of character obey when their parents give them an instruction.

There are some ground rules for you as a parent if you want to make this work. First, don't ask your kids to do something unless you really want them to do it. Don't ask them unless you're willing to go to the wall for it. Otherwise, don't give the command. Don't ask them to do a thousand things, but when you do ask them to do something, you'd better be willing to enforce it. If you give orders and then don't follow through, your instructions will be meaningless in the future.

Tell your kids, "I'll never ask you anything to embarrass you. I'll never ask you anything that will compromise your integrity. When I ask you to do something, I have a reason. I'm not just jerking you around. There's a reason for what I do, but you don't need to know every reason."

I remember when I was a kid, my daddy was a strong disciplinarian. He laughed a lot, and I liked that about him, but when Daddy asked you to do something the second time, that was one time too many which resulted in my being disciplined—but that saved my life when I was a young boy.

We used to go out hunting for salamanders to use for trout fishing bait. One day my dad and I were looking in a mountain stream in a little place called Turtle Town in east Tennessee. We had to get down in the stream where there was about six inches of water and then we'd lift up the rocks, because the salamanders would lie under them where the water was shallow.

The problem was that the copperheads liked to lie on rocks in those little streams in the middle of the day, so you didn't want to wait too late to go looking for bait. To get one of those little salamanders, you had to be really quiet and slow and lift up the rock enough to get the dirt stirred up—and there underneath the rock would be a salamander. When you touched his tail, he'd run right up in your hand.

Well, that day I was bent over, picking up rocks, and all of a sudden my daddy hollered at me from about thirty yards upstream: "Jump, Son! Jump!"

I didn't say, "What?" I just came up out of the water! Now I was five years old, but by age five I had learned something: When Daddy said something, it meant now! So I jumped. The problem was that I jumped the wrong way.

A copperhead had crawled up on the rock behind me and was getting ready to nail me from behind. When I jumped, I jumped back instead of jumping out. Now the copperhead's the nastiest snake ever made. Rattlesnakes are nice snakes because they'll let you know when they're upset. A copperhead won't let you know. He just loves for you to get close to him.

When Daddy yelled, "Jump!" I came up backwards and landed right on that rock, right on top of that copperhead! *Boom!* My little Keds tennis shoes nailed that snake to that rock, but his tail kept slapping at my ankles.

Daddy came running, grabbed me under my armpits, and sent me flying through the air! I felt like a NASA rocket! I hit that riverbank and looked back at that snake. My daddy was doing a war dance on it and throwing rocks at it. He finally got out his .22 pistol and killed it.

The point of the story is that Daddy had taught me obedience. He'd taught me that there may come a time when he'd ask me to do something that would save my life. He'd always told me, "When I ask you to do something, do it. We'll talk about it later."

That was good parenting. We can learn something from that. We shouldn't allow our children to sit and have a conversation with us when we ask them to do something. On the other hand, we shouldn't be asking them to do stupid things either.

We should be able to say, "Darlin', if I ask you to do something, you've got to do it now. Even if it's a mundane chore, like closing the door, opening a window, or turning off a light, I need it done and I need it done now." We should be able to stand in our authority and say, "I'm the adult. I'm not your servant. I'm not your buddy. You need to listen and obey."

A Good Work Ethic

Second Thessalonians 3:10 says, "If you don't work, you don't eat." Any successful family knows this. Even people in the world understand this. I love to read stories about people like the Fords and the Rockefellers and how they trained their children to take over their businesses. Most of those great entrepreneurs taught their kids the value of hard work.

To have an advantage in this life, our kids have to have a strong work ethic. To instill that in them, we have to give them chores at home. It doesn't have to be a lot. You can have your kids do about fifteen minutes of manual labor every weekday and forty-five minutes on Saturdays. The rest of the day, just have a big time. Don't box them in and make them feel like you're the devil hovering over them all day. Give them some time to play too.

You can say, "Hey, we've got forty-five minutes, and I've got five things I need you to do. Come on. Let's get after it, and then the rest of the day we can have a great time." I wish somebody would come and motivate me like that sometimes! Wouldn't that be great?

Earning Money and Spending It Wisely

For children to learn how to earn money, we can't give them everything. I give my kids some money because God's a giver, but most of the time I give them a chance to earn it. And they don't earn money for making the bed or washing the dishes. If they eat off the dish, they wash the dish. If they use the toilet, they clean the toilet. If they wear the clothes, they wash the clothes.

Don't let your kids grow up to be twenty years old and still not know how to turn on the washing machine. If they can run the computer, they can run that washing machine. If they've got the computer working, they can work the three buttons on the dryer. If they're having a tough time sorting the clothes, paint Star Wars pictures on the front of the machines. Make a game out of it. Make schematics and pin them up in the laundry room: "See, these colors go together. These don't."

These are things they should be doing for their regular chores, as part of the family, but you can help them do more than the basics to earn some extra money. And when they start earning money, you need to teach them to spend it wisely. Don't let your kids just go out and spend their money without your knowing about it. You can't train them if all you do is say, "Well, it's your money. Do what you want to." That's wrong. They won't learn anything that way.

You need to tell them, "I don't care if you earned it. I gave it to you, and as long as you're in my house, I'm going to train you how to spend that money wisely. No, you're not buying that. That's goofy."

It's important to show our kids examples of wise spending. When they were little, I'd take my kids with me when we bought cereal, and they'd say, "Buy the bigger box!" But that's not always the best choice, so we'd look down at the little bar code, and I'd ask them, "How much is that per ounce?" That label is always ankle, or knee high, but my kids could read it. So I'd teach them how to comparison shop and how to spend money wisely.

We also need to teach our kids how to *save* the money that they earn. Proverbs 6:6 KJV says, "Go to the ant, thou sluggard; consider her ways, and be wise." An ant's got enough sense to know when to store up something. So should we.

My kids have been saving money all their lives. They save money for two events every year: family vacation and Christmas. They have their own money for those things because I don't let them squander it during the rest of the year. I make sure it's in a savings account that they can't touch without my signature.

Our kids also need to learn to *give* out of the money that they earn. I want my kids to learn to be givers. God loves a cheerful giver, so I teach them to give.

Teaching our kids to earn money and use it wisely is an important way to build their character.

Common Courtesy

Kids ought to learn courtesy at home by obeying us and by our example. This is so important, but most often it's not taught. All these little courtesies add up to a lot of godly character.

1. We need to teach our kids to say, "Please," "Thank you," "Yes, sir," and "No, sir." People think it's old-fashioned, but courtesy will never get old. Our kids

are going to work for somebody who's going to want to hear these words someday.

2. We need to teach our kids courtesy in their bathroom manners. This is a big one. Nobody wants to marry somebody who doesn't have any bathroom manners. I don't want to get too graphic here, but we need to teach our kids to be meticulous and tidy up the toilet, the floor, and the counter before they come out of that bathroom.

3. We need to teach our kids to keep their noise level down when it could disturb others. For example, when we're at a hotel swimming in the pool and some nice elderly people come and sit down, I say, "Get the noise level down."

They look at me like they're brain dead and ask, "Why?"

I point to the people, and they say, "Okay, we'll stop."

We need to train our kids to respect the people around them.

4. We need to teach our kids not to pop gum when anybody is around. And don't let them stick it anywhere! If you've ever gotten gum stuck on the bottom of your shoe, you know the significance of what I'm saying.

5. We need to teach our kids to always knock on a door when it's closed and ask permission to come in before opening it up. That will get you embarrassed. Enough said.

6. We need to teach them to be courteous and respond promptly if they've been invited to go somewhere. My kids used to say, "I don't know if I'll go or not. Let me find out if Billy Jean's going." I'd tell them, "If the invitation comes in the mail today, you're going to respond today. You're not going to make somebody have to buy an extra hot dog because you showed up on their doorstep at the last minute."

7. We need to teach our kids the courtesy of returning anything they borrow on time and in good condition.

8. We should teach our kids to be on time and to leave on time. Kids don't know when to leave. There's nothing worse than somebody hanging around when everything's over and everyone else has left. I've had people come to the house— people with college degrees—who just didn't know when to leave.

Yawn, "I'm glad you like it here, but we sure need to go to bed." But they're just kind of hanging out, and I'm thinking, *This is not the bed and breakfast. You don't have a room here. Go home!*

9. We need to teach our kids to walk up and down stairs and through hallways quietly. Sometime you might go to a nice hotel, and you don't want your kids tearing up and down the hall and getting everybody bent out of shape.

10. We need to teach them not to leave things for the next person to do. Who's supposed to clean out the lint screen in the dryer? Why is it that nobody wants to do that? I tell my kids that every time they open that dryer door, they need to pull that lint screen out and clean it. We should teach our kids to take responsibility and do what needs to be done when they see it.

11. We need to teach our kids to obey *all* signs at *all* times. Signs have a purpose.

12. We need to teach our kids to keep their feet off the furniture. I've seen kids come into a high school after we've spent millions of dollars to build new facilities, and they stick their feet up on the back of the seat in front of them. I think, *You must live in a*

barn, because you did that so naturally; it was like you didn't even think. You do that at home, don't you?

13. We also have to teach them the courtesy of giving up their seat to somebody who needs it more than they do. I fly through Dallas a lot, and on the "puddle-jumper" flights, they have these busses to take you to the planes from the main gate. I've been astounded how women with babies or the elderly will get in, and grown businessmen with their suits and briefcases will just sit on their rumps and not even think about getting up! They'll just look up with their cell phones and keep doing their deals. I think, *You may be dressed up on the outside, but on the inside you're a sorry dog!*

14. We should teach our kids not to groom themselves in public. They shouldn't be picking their teeth, fiddling with their fingernails, combing their hair, or spitting if anyone else is around. Wait till you get in your car or go to the restroom to do that. You look like a monkey picking on himself.

15. We should teach our kids to respect books—no matter who wrote them.

16. We need to teach our kids to respect public property. That means no graffiti. When we built our new church building, it wasn't twenty-four hours before some kids had scribbled something on it. What was in their minds when they did that? Nothing! They took something we all gave money to build, and they just had to write something on it that wasn't even intelligent. Don't let your kids mess up what someone else has labored for.

17. We need to teach our kids not to cut in line. Years ago I got so embarrassed at a big pastor's conference. I highly respect the pastor who invited us, but he apparently didn't like standing still very much. It was time for a meal, and he said, "Come on. Let's get in line." We got in about two-thirds of the way back in the line, and people were lining up behind us. He said, "Hey, I see somebody I know. Come here a minute. I want to introduce you to someone."

Of course, the person he knew was right up at the head of the line. We got up there and stood there a few seconds while the pastor I was with waited to introduce me. The guy he knew was talking to somebody else. Within thirty seconds, the pastor I was with had gotten us to the front of the line with a simple, "How are you doing? Nice to meet you. Do you mind if we stay here?"

I felt like dirt! I was so embarrassed! Elderly people and kids were in that line, and I was thinking, *Why are we in such a hurry? It's just food. It'll still be here if we wait.* Cutting in line is really rude. If you don't have the patience to wait your turn, just get up and go home.

18. Teach your kids to say they're sorry if they dial a wrong number on the telephone. Never just hang up. (If you do, may God give you a hundred-fold return on that.) When somebody does that to you, you wonder, *Was that an emergency? Was it one of my kids?* Your day is shot because you wonder who tried to call you. The caller's day isn't shot. They just made a mistake but don't have enough hair on their lip to admit it. Teach your kids to say, "I'm sorry, I dialed the wrong number."

19. We need to teach our kids to be courteous and careful when they're driving. They need to do this not only out of consideration for others, but for safety's sake. Teach your kids to be courteous drivers.

Live Peaceably at Home

We've talked about the ways we can teach our kids to be courteous, and right along with that is the ability to live peaceably with others, especially with their brothers and sisters. If your kids can't get along at home with their own brothers and sisters, they're going to be wild when they go out into the world. Don't allow any knock-down-drag-out fighting in your household. Make that an offense punishable with the rod. If you don't want to be down at the principal's office all the time because your kids keep getting into fights, teach them to live peaceably with others, especially at home.

There are four specific areas that you can work on with your children to help them get along with their siblings.

1. Teach your kids to respect each other's possessions or else they're going to be stealing and fighting over stuff. Sometimes one of my daughters will come out in her sister's clothes. "Is that your dress?" "Is that your blouse?" "Are those your shoes?" "I don't think so."

"Well, I'll ask her if I can wear it later."

"No, you're not asking anyone later. Take it off. I don't care if all your stuff is dirty. You should have washed your stuff last night."

2. On the other side of the coin, brothers and sisters do have to be taught to share their property. Now that seems like a flip-flop from what I just said, but it isn't. Siblings should be *willing* to share, but they need to *ask* first. Otherwise, your kids will go to college and feel like they can wear anything out of their roommate's closet.

3. Your children need to be taught to forgive and to ask for forgiveness. You've got to teach your children to let things go—and to own up to their own mistakes.

Honesty

4. You don't want your kids to cheat and lie. If they do, no one will want to be around them. No one will ever trust them. I don't care how smart they are, they've got to be honest. Did you know that the number-one trait most employers say they want in their employees is honesty? They're not looking for geniuses. They're not looking for blue-chippers. They're not looking for people who can walk on water. They just want to know, "Will you show up?

Will you do the job? Will you not steal from me?"
Integrity will take you a long way in the workplace.

Character Matters

Your example, your expectations, and your discipline
will help build character in your kids. Use this chapter as
a reference to pinpoint the strengths that you want to
build in your kids, and then ask the Holy Spirit to help
you do it. He'll lead you to the Scriptures you need for
the job. He'll also show you how to make the job fun,
which leads us to the last thing that no kid should leave
home without.

8

A Sense of Humor

The eighth and final thing that no kid should leave home without gets people a long way in life. In fact, if our kids are going to have an advantage in life, they've got to have this. It's a sense of humor.

Maybe you never thought about it, but God wants us to have a sense of humor. God is a fun God. If you didn't think He was, you wouldn't want to go to Heaven. I wouldn't. People want to go to the amusement park because it's supposed to be fun. And we want to go to Heaven because we know it's a happy place—and that's because God is fun.

Here are eight Scriptures to prove it to you.

A merry heart doeth good like a medicine: but a broken spirit drieth the bones.

Proverbs 17:22 KJV

All the days of the afflicted are evil: but he that is of a merry heart hath a continual feast.

Proverbs 15:15 KJV

A merry heart maketh a cheerful countenance: but by sorrow of the heart the spirit is broken.

Proverbs 15:13 KJV

...The joy of the Lord is your strength.

Nehemiah 8:10

Let thy priests be clothed with righteousness; and let thy saints shout for joy.

Psalm 132:9 KJV

...Enter thou into the joy of thy lord.

Matthew 25:21 KJV

These things have I spoken unto you, that my joy might remain in you, and that your joy might be full.

John 15:11 KJV

Yet I will rejoice in the LORD, I will be joyful in God my Savior.

Habakkuk 3:18

Humor Is a Choice

A sense of humor is not the ability to make fun of someone else. That's called jesting, and the Bible condemns those who jest. (Eph. 5:4.) However, the Bible is full of stories of people who were able to laugh their way out of trouble. When David thought everything he owned had been destroyed and his own men were about to kill him, he encouraged himself in the Lord. (1 Sam. 30:6.) He rejoiced. He made himself glad by thinking about everything God had done for him, and it gave him the strength to go on the offense against the enemy.

When the Bible says, "I will rejoice" (Ps. 118:24), that's a decision, not a feeling. People who have a sense of humor choose to take a difficult situation and make it fun. They'll make it funny and they'll rise above it.

I've heard stories of people who literally laughed their way out of terminal illness. They bought a bunch of funny movies, and watched them over and over and laughed their way out of dying. Many doctors believe that laughing releases chemicals in our bodies that will actually speed the healing process. They've simply "discovered" what the Bible has said all along, that laughter "does good, like medicine" (Prov. 17:22 NKJV).

Having a sense of humor is a choice. You can't wait until something makes you do it. You just have to say, "I'm going to find the funny part of this." I love to laugh. My family loves to laugh. We have more funny videos and DVDs than anyone I know. If it's funny, we own it. We have made a choice to keep our household full of joy.

My Prayer for My Family

Years ago as a young husband and father I heard a series on the home at a Christian businessmen's meeting. The speaker quoted John 17 and discussed the three things that Jesus prayed just before He went to the cross.

1. Unity

First, He prayed, "Father, I'm praying for everybody alive and everybody yet to be born. Make everybody one together with You, just as You and I are one." (See v. 11, also 22-23.) Jesus prayed that our relationships in the Body of Christ and with the Father would be as close as the relationship He has with His Father. That's the way I want my family to be: as close as Jesus and His Father are.

So I started praying that over my family a long time ago, and I still do it today. "Father, I want unity in my home, not just as members of the Body of Christ, but as a family. I've seen lots of homes that were destroyed by strife. I don't want that. I want my family to be a family of unity. No division. No strife. We can find solutions to problems without tearing the family apart."

That doesn't mean we get along with everybody all the time. We still bump heads on stuff. We know how to get back into fellowship and get back together again. We're a close family because we're *for* one another.

2. Joy

The second thing Jesus prayed was, "Let My joy be made manifest in them." You can't even fathom this. Jesus prayed, "May they be known as a people of laughter and a people of joy." (See v. 13.) That's what I want for my family: that we would be known for our laughter and joy.

So I prayed that we'd be a family of laughter. Did you know that on that old show *The Dating Game*, the number-one, most-often-desired character trait in a mate was a great sense of humor? Even unbelievers want that.

Even ungodly people have enough sense to say, "I don't want to be married to somebody who's an old fuddy-duddy, stick-in-the-mud. I want to marry somebody who will be fun." Remember God is a fun God. He wants us to be happy.

In our family we choose entertainment that will make us happy. We'd much rather be laughing than crying. We don't go to very many movies. I usually wait until they're out on DVD and then check them out before I let my kids watch them. However, I can still remember the one show we went to that was supposed to be a great family movie. We sat down in the theater, and ten minutes into that thing I thought, *I'm depressed.*

One of the kids said, "Well, just give it a minute."

I said, "No, I already gave it ten or twelve minutes, and it's getting worse. This is no good. We're out of here. Get your popcorn, and come on!"

"Where are we going?"

"Somewhere else. Somewhere that's fun." We went to the local amusement park and had a good time.

If we're going to have family time, I want to have a good time. We're not going to sit around and bawl and squall through a movie.

"But it's a true story."

"I don't care if it is true. It's not true for me!" I'd been praying for a family of laughter and joy, and that wasn't going to get us there. I don't want my family to be depressed. I want to us to be laughing every chance we get.

3. Victory Over Evil

Third, Jesus prayed, "Don't take them out of this world, but keep them from the evil that's in the world." That's another thing I want for my family: victory on this Earth. (See v. 15.)

So I prayed that God would keep us from the evil in this world. We're in the world but not of it. We're winning battles together because we're laughing together. We can laugh our way through life, because the joy of the Lord is our strength.

When circumstances get tough, we can choose to rejoice like Paul and Silas. They sang a song of joy in a rat-filled prison. (Acts 16:25.) They'd been beaten and bloodied. They were sitting in the dark. Rats were crawling up their legs. In the middle of all that, Paul said, "Hey, Silas, I feel a song coming on...." Rattling those chains, they just began to clap their hands and sing. How do you think they did that? They made a choice. Paul said, "I'm going to sing me a song," and Silas said, "Hey, that's a great idea!"

I'll bet they harmonized and got louder the longer they sang. I guarantee you the anointing hit them like a lightning bolt. Before the power of God ever rattled that cage, it rattled them and they started to rock and roll! Then an earthquake hit, the prison doors opened, and a whole bunch of people—including the jailer—all got saved. (Acts 16:25-30.) Whatever terrible situations we're in, we can choose to praise God and keep moving right into victory.

It's a Choice

We just have to choose to say, "This is the day the Lord has made. I'm going to rejoice and be glad in it. I'm going to have a good time today." (See Ps. 118:24.) You'll be surprised what that Word will do for you and your kids. It will point your children toward success in life day after day. A sense of humor will put them over in life, and they'll be full of the power of God because His joy will be their strength. Let's be the salt and light God called us to be. Let's go through life encouraging others, being a blessing and leaving people better than we find them. We need to remind our kids that life is not a destination. Life is a journey. Let's enjoy the journey. Let's have people want to ask us about the hope that is in us. That's why a great sense of humor is the final thing they just shouldn't leave home without.

Conclusion

Eight things.

We've learned eight things that we can put in our kids to give them an advantage in life.

The best part about it is that every one of these things is something I can *choose* to do.

First, I can choose to have a strong sense of self-worth. I can say, "I'm going to start seeing myself the way Jesus sees me. To do that, I'm going to put my face in the Bible and believe that what God says about me is true."

Second, I'm going to get some vision. How? I'm going to ask God to show me and my kids what He has called us to do. I can pray, "I want revelation, Lord. Tell me what You want me to do." (Deut. 29:29.)

Third, I'm going to say, "I don't hate math. I *love* math. I don't care if I flunked it four years in a row. I love math, and math loves me. I'm good with numbers. Let's get out the pencil and one of those calculators that will calculate interest. Everybody else has been making money off of me; now I'm going to start making some for myself."

Fourth, I can choose to be organized and to manage my time. I'm going to speak God's Word over myself in the areas where I have been lacking, and I'm going to work on my organizational skills—and practice them until they are habits. I'm going to get control of my time. I can keep time management simple by just writing everything down. When I start writing it down, I'll be well on my way to being consistently organized.

Fifth, I'm going to be teachable. I'm not afraid of learning. I love to learn new things. I'm going to humble myself and ask lots of questions. I'm desiring and acquiring knowledge every day.

Sixth, I can develop good communication skills and learn how to talk to people. I'm going to find a good book on etiquette and put it with the sixth chapter of this book and study it. Then I'll be a great communicator.

Seventh, I can choose to be a person of character. I'm going to let Jesus develop my character. I'm going to do what's right even when nobody's looking because Somebody is looking and He's writing it all down.

Finally, I can choose to have a great sense of humor. I'm going to choose to be happy. Nobody's got it all together. But I can laugh at myself and laugh my way through life. If I can do that, I can go anywhere and do anything. The joy of the Lord is my strength.

God sets opportunities before us every day. I pray that this book will give you an opportunity to teach your family how to grow into everything that God has created them to be.

Lean on God's strength and seek His wisdom in the Word. God is counting on you to teach your kids what you've learned and to give them what they need for the days ahead.

—Joe McGee

Endnotes

1 A Sense of Self-Worth

[1] http://www.catinthehat.org/history.htm

[2] http://www.poets.org/poet.php/prmPID/192

2 A Love of Math

[1] http://www.jewishvirtuallibrary.org/jsource/Judaism/jewpop.html

[2] http://www.newfoundationspubl.org/healingp.htm

[3] http://en.wikipedia.org/wiki/Rosenwald_Fund

5 A Teachable Spirit

[1] http://www.obituariestoday.com/Obituaries/ObitShow.cfm?Obituary_ID=30082&section=pin

Prayer of Salvation

God loves you—no matter who you are, no matter what your past. God loves you so much that He gave His one and only begotten Son for you. The Bible tells us that "...whoever believes in him shall not perish but have eternal life" (John 3:16 NIV). Jesus laid down His life and rose again so that we could spend eternity with Him in Heaven and experience His absolute best on Earth. If you would like to receive Jesus into your life, say the following prayer out loud and mean it from your heart.

Heavenly Father, I come to You admitting that I am a sinner. Right now, I choose to turn away from sin, and I ask You to cleanse me of all unrighteousness. I believe that Your Son, Jesus, died on the cross to take away my sins. I also believe that He rose again from the dead so that I might be forgiven of my sins and made righteous through faith in Him. I call upon the name of Jesus Christ to be the Savior and Lord of my life. Jesus, I choose to follow You and ask that You fill me with the power of the Holy Spirit. I declare that right now I am a child of God. I am free from sin and full of the righteousness of God. I am saved in Jesus' name. Amen.

If you prayed this prayer to receive Jesus Christ as your Savior for the first time, please contact us on the Web at **www.harrisonhouse.com** to receive a free book.

Or you may write to us at

Harrison House

P.O. Box 35035

Tulsa, Oklahoma 74153

About the Author

Joe McGee, minister, author, national conference speaker, father, and former school administrator, is the founder and director of Faith for Families and Joe McGee Ministries.

Joe presents some of the most entertaining yet practical and insightful teaching on the family available today. Packing more into one sermon than anyone you've ever met, Joe gives insights into relationships that will open up scriptural secrets and common-sense applications to powerfully change marriages, families, and lives.

Joe mixes years of personal experience with principles of God's Word to bring pointed but humorous illustrations that challenge people to become what God intended them to be. His laugh-and-learn approach removes every barrier and provides a refreshing point of view, a new hope for better families, and a deeper commitment to obey the Word of God.

A husband of over thirty-five years and father of six children, Joe has invested the past thirty years in training people from all walks of life in family, marriage, and parenting issues.

Joe, his wife, Denise, and their family make their home in Tulsa, Oklahoma.

To contact Joe McGee please write to:

Joe McGee

P.O. Box 691498

Tulsa, Oklahoma 74169-1498

www.joemcgeeministries.com

Please include your prayer requests
and comments when you write.

Fast. Easy.
Convenient.

For the latest Harrison House product information and author news, look no further than your computer. All the details on our powerful, life-changing products are just a click away. New releases, E-mail subscriptions, Podcasts, testimonies, monthly specials—find it all in one place. Visit harrisonhouse.com today!

harrisonhouse

The Harrison House Vision

Proclaiming the truth and the power

Of the Gospel of Jesus Christ

With excellence;

Challenging Christians to

Live victoriously,

Grow spiritually,

Know God intimately.